William V

Mark Williamson has been involved in training emerging leaders for the last eight years, he currently serves as a director of One Rock, leads a Café Church in south west London, and is a part of the Prayer for London team. He has also authored a biography on John Wesley as part of the Remarkable Lives series.

William Wilberforce:
Achieving the Impossible

Mark Williamson

Authentic

20 19 18 17 16 15 14   7 6 5 4 3 2 1

First published in 2014 by Authentic Media Limited
52 Presley Way, Crownhill, Milton Keynes, MK8 0ES.
authenticmedia.co.uk

British Library Cataloguing in Publication Data
A catalogue record for this book is available from the British Library
ISBN: 978-1-78078-063-4   978-1-78078-065-8 (e-book)

Cover design by Paul Airy (designleft.co.uk)
Printed and bound by CPI Group (UK) Ltd., Croydon, CR0 4YY

Contents

Preface –
One Rock International

This book is part of a series that has been developed by One Rock. Each book is a biography of a different missionary leader. One Rock is passionate about empowering spiritual leaders to fulfil God's vision for their lives, and so make a kingdom difference wherever they are in the world.

Throughout the history of Christianity, there have been countless examples of missionary leaders who allowed God to do incredible things through them. However, many of their stories and lives are unknown to this generation. These books aim to remind us of all that God has done through individuals in the past, and so give us a greater expectation of what he might do through us in the present and future.

Each book tells the life story of an individual, and comprehensively covers all of their most famous writings and quotes. Each aims to be high on information, brief in length and readable in style.

At the end of each chapter there are summaries with key points that show leaders in the twenty-first century what they can learn from the people of the past. These points are grouped into the four curriculum areas in which One Rock provides resources for people: Spiritual Formation,

Discerning Vision, Leadership Skills and Mission Skills. Each of these is denoted by the following icons:

 Spiritual Formation

 Discerning Vision

 Leadership Skills

 **Mission Skills**

We hope these books challenge, inspire and inform your leadership for Jesus. For more information and resources, visit <u>onerockinternational.com</u>.

Foreword

Another biography of William Wilberforce! What is it about this remarkable and complex man that continues to fascinate and demand our attention? The enormity of the evil against which he campaigned so effectively, winning against all the odds? Certainly! The fact that he lived at a time of huge social and political upheaval? Yes, that as well!

He was politically conservative, and the beneficiary of a system that denied the overwhelming majority the vote and gave huge power to an elite of wealthy and privileged men. Universal suffrage was certainly not a cause he espoused. Yet he championed human rights and took up a cause which those strongly vested interests used all their power and might to uphold. The slave owners bought up every rotten borough and member of parliament that they could lay their hands on. This fact, however, and his undoubted capacity to mobilize the power of mass action, never seems to have caused him to become, himself, politically radical. He was very much a 'man of the establishment'. But this did not cause him to accept the established wisdom of the day.

His was a life lived to the full. He sought all the worldly pleasures that were available to a young man of his class and time. And yet was acutely aware of the fleeting nature of these, turning away from them as he grew older, but without ever becoming a prig and a sermonising bore. He was an acutely social person to whom friendships were important. These enduring friendships, not least but not only with the great office holders of the day, proved invaluable to his causes and the achievement of his ambitions. Yet these ambitions never seemed to involve seeking personal office, of which his undoubted talents and energy might have made him the beneficiary. It is all of these at times contradictory elements of his personality that make him for me a subject worthy of continuing study and reflection. He was and still remains to an extent an enigma. His remarks towards the end of his life, in which he reflects on the fact that he felt himself in some ways unknown even to his friends, give one a sense that he was perhaps aware of this. We are all to a certain extent of course profoundly alone and unknowable except to God. It is not easy to accept this. Wilberforce seems to have embraced it.

I have recently embarked upon a series of walks in a stretch of the countryside along the shore between Dover and Folkestone; places Wilberforce knew well and where he took sanctuary during his not infrequent bouts of nervous exhaustion and illness. I try to imagine how these in some instances unchanged aspects of sky, land and sea, and the passing marine traffic, must have invoked in his mind those horrifying images of the Atlantic Passage which inspired him to ever greater efforts against the 'abominable trade'. The terror of those wrenched from their ancestral homelands, in the stinking bowels of the slave ships on stormy seas, and the brutalizing effect on all touched by and engaged upon the slave trade was very real to him. He had a profoundly sympathetic imagination. This is brought alive in his impassioned speeches to an, at first, sceptical and largely hostile House of Commons.

His oratorical abilities linked with an acute political and strategic sensibility made him a formidable operator.

He was not of course a lone operator. He forged powerful alliances at every level of society. He seems to have recognized early on the need in any activist campaign to reach out and embrace broad and at times disparate elements from which it is necessary to forge a common platform, built upon a basis upon which all can agree. This requires patience and an ability to reach out beyond creed or faction and compromise without undermining the fundamental integrity of all concerned. How rare a form of leadership this is. How desperately today, in a world riven by divisions and fanaticism of a hitherto unimaginable form and scale, it is needed now. The hour found its man in William Wilberforce. His was a personality and style of leadership that was shaped by a profound and transformatory faith. 'Amazing Grace' indeed!

Mark Williamson's eminently readable biography of Wilberforce provides not just a pocket guide to a complex man whose gifts and calling were brought to bear at the very heart of public and political affairs, but to the living of a Christian life. Wilberforce's brand of Christian activism is a much needed antidote to the aggressive secularism of our age, and an example to all who might otherwise be tempted by despair at the way things are to retreat into a sort of pietism that turns its back on the world and its challenges. There is a real alternative as Wilberforce magnificently demonstrates in a life lived without fear of engagement with thorny issues in difficult places. We face all too many of these today in a world which often seems ill-equipped to handle them. The language of faith is widely disparaged in our society, and vision and values seem in short supply. Williamson demonstrates in this usefully annotated book how Wilberforce's life and the lessons to be learnt from it can help us all practically to make a difference in these times as we try to follow in the footsteps of Jesus of Nazareth.

The Rt Hon The Lord Boateng, PC DL
'Equiano's Reach'
Sandgate,
Kent
September 2014

1

A Misspent Youth: 1759–1779

Born into a wealthy family in 1759, William Wilberforce's childhood seemed the perfect preparation for a rich gentleman to live a life of idleness. A brush with 'serious religion' was narrowly avoided, leaving him free to pursue pleasure and indulgence.

A Merchant Family

Wilberforce was born in Hull, Yorkshire, on 24 August 1759, the only son of Robert and Elizabeth Wilberforce. He had two older sisters, Elizabeth and Sarah, and a younger one called Anne. His grandfather, Alderman William Wilberforce, had made money trading goods from Hull with other coastal cities in the Netherlands, northern Germany, Scandinavia and the Baltic region. He did so well at it that young William Wilberforce grew up two generations later in one of the wealthiest and most influential families in the town.

Wilberforce was a weak and sickly child, but was sent to the local grammar school as a boy. It was a good school, with headmaster Joseph Milner considered something of an intellectual prodigy. It was here that Wilberforce started to show promise of his later skills as a public speaker. Milner's brother later remembered, 'Even then his elocution was so remarkable that we used to set him upon a table, and make him read aloud as an example to the other boys.'[1]

It was a happy childhood, but was interrupted in spring 1768 when Wilberforce's father and older sister Elizabeth died within weeks of each other. His mother felt unable to cope in raising the boy on her own, so 9-year-old William was sent to live with his aunt and uncle in London.

Wimbledon

Aunt Hannah and Uncle William Wilberforce had a town house in London, and a family home eight miles away in Wimbledon. The young William spent holidays in Wimbledon, and term time boarding in neighbouring Putney, a poor school where he complained he learned nothing compared to Hull grammar.

What Wilberforce did learn during his holidays in Wimbledon was 'serious religion'. His aunt and uncle were both converts to the relatively new sect of Methodism. This was viewed with extreme suspicion by many in the Church of England (and the wider country) for causing people to become a little too zealous about Christianity. Aunt Hannah and Uncle William were friends with George Whitefield, one of the great leaders and preachers of the Methodist revival. Whitefield would stay with the family when in the area. John Newton, a former slave ship captain turned evangelical Anglican vicar, was also friends with them. These two men, and the religion of Aunt Hannah and Uncle William, started to have a profound influence on the young William.

Wimbledon Life

My father's elder brother, who had married a sister of Mr John Thornton, had previously settled in London. He had a house in St James's Place, and a villa at Wimbledon. I was much with them. My aunt was an admirer of Whitefield's preaching, and kept up a friendly connection with the early Methodists; and I often accompanied her and my uncle to church and to chapel. I was warmly attached to them both. They had no children, and I was to be their heir. Under these influences my mind was, even in those early days, much interested and impressed by the subject of religion. In what degree these impressions were genuine I can hardly determine, but at least I may venture to say that I was sincere. From the tenor of my letters, some of which are still in existence, my friends in Yorkshire became alarmed with the idea that I was in danger of becoming a Methodist. My mother was a very worthy woman, one of Archbishop Tillotson's school, who always went to church prayers on Wednesdays and Fridays, but at this time had no just conception of the spiritual nature and aim of Christianity. The apprehensions I have mentioned brought her up to town to fetch me away.[2]

His mother, well aware of the social stigma attached to Methodism, knew enough of 'serious religion' to offer sarcastic comfort to the couple who had their young heir taken away from them. 'You should not fear. If it be a work of grace, you know it cannot fail.'[3] But if this thought brought any comfort to his aunt and uncle, it provided no solace for Wilberforce. 'I deeply felt the parting for I loved them as parents: indeed, I was almost heart-broken at the separation.'[4]

Back to Hull

Wilberforce was brought back to Hull to be rescued from a lifetime of Methodism and ridicule, and grandfather Alderman Wilberforce gave instructions for the remainder of his education. 'Billy shall travel with Milner as soon as he is of age; but if Billy turns Methodist he shall not have a sixpence of mine.'[5]

But a return to Hull grammar school and the care of Joseph Milner was not to be. The plague of Methodism had now reached Hull, and Milner himself had joined their ranks. Rather than send Wilberforce back into another hotbed of serious Christianity, the family enrolled him at a school in Pocklington, twenty-one miles away from Hull. They also gave the young boy a crash course in theatre, card-playing, and all the other worldly pursuits that were so condemned by the Methodists, to make sure any lingering traces of religion were beaten out of him.

Hull Social Life

It [Hull] was then as gay a place as could be found out of London. The theatre, balls, great suppers, and card-parties, were the delight of the principal families in the town. The usual dinner hour was two o'clock, and at six they met at sumptuous suppers. This mode of life was at first distressing to me, but by degrees I acquired a relish for it, and became as thoughtless as the rest. As grandson of one of the principal inhabitants, I was every where invited and caressed: my voice and love of music made me still more acceptable. The religious impressions which I had gained at Wimbledon continued for a considerable time after my return to Hull, but my friends spared no pains to stifle them. I might almost say, that no pious parent ever laboured more to impress a beloved child with sentiments of piety, than they did to give me a taste for the world and its diversions.[6]

When he was thirty-eight Wilberforce looked back on this period and saw how God had used it to bring him to a role in public life where he could be useful, but at the time he slowly became more and more immersed in the usual social life of a young man preparing for university.

Rescued from Methodism

My mother's taking me from my uncle's when about twelve or thirteen and then completely a Methodist, has probably been the means of my being connected with political men and becoming useful in life. If I had staid with my uncle I should probably have been a bigoted despised Methodist.[7]

Cambridge

Hull may have been a lively place, but it was clearly nothing compared to life as an undergraduate at Cambridge University, where Wilberforce arrived aged seventeen in October 1776.

First Night at University

I was introduced on the very first night of my arrival, to as licentious a set of men as can well be conceived. They drank hard, and their conversation was even worse than their lives. I lived amongst them for some time, though I never relished their society ... often indeed I was horror-struck at their conduct ... and after the first year I shook off in great measure my connexion with them.[8]

Wilberforce did make and retain many friends at Cambridge though. As a young gentleman with plenty of money and a talent for singing and witty conversation he was never short of company. One fellow student who became a great friend in his adult life was Thomas Gisborne, who remembered Wilberforce as the life and soul of any party, but not someone given to serious study.

Gisborne's Recollections

There was no one at all like him for powers of entertainment. Always fond of repartee and discussion, he seemed entirely free from conceit and vanity ... There was always a great Yorkshire pie in his rooms, and all were welcome to partake of it. My rooms and his were back to back, and often when I was raking out my fire at ten o'clock, I heard his melodious voice calling aloud to me to come and sit with him before I went to bed. It was a dangerous thing to do, for his amusing conversation was sure to keep me up so late, that I was behind-hand the next morning.[9]

Wilberforce was certainly not a conscientious student.

Lazy Student Days

Whilst my companions were reading hard and attending lectures, card parties and idle amusements consumed my time. The tutors would often say within my hearing, that 'they were mere saps, but that I did all by talent.' This was poison to a mind constituted like mine.[10]

He spent four years at Cambridge, barely studying, but doing enough to just get through his degree. He wasn't as wild as many others in his behaviour, but had definitely left behind the Methodism picked up in Wimbledon. 'I certainly did not then think and act as I do now, but I was so far from what the world calls licentious, that I was rather complimented on being better than young men in general.'[11]

A Misspent Youth

Key Learning Points

Spiritual Formation

Adults influence children. The influence of Wilberforce's aunt, uncle, Whitefield and Newton drew him closer to God. His mother and grandfather pushed him away from God.

Prioritize education. Wilberforce regretted in later life wasting his student years and not learning enough.

Discerning Vision

God can work through all life's circumstances. A childhood spent in two different worlds enabled Wilberforce to relate to both groups as an adult.

Gifts can be discerned from an early age. Wilberforce's skill of public speaking was apparent even from the age of nine.

A Man of Consequence: 1779–1784

Following university Wilberforce decided to pursue a career in parliament, and was elected as MP for Hull. Within five years he had progressed to represent one of the most prestigious seats in the country, and was best friends with the Prime Minister.

Election to Parliament

By Wilberforce's final year at Cambridge, both Alderman William Wilberforce and Uncle William Wilberforce had died. Wilberforce was therefore sole heir to the family business and the property portfolio. The business had for many years been run by Abel Smith, employed as a manager by the family. Wilberforce had no interest in remaining in Hull to become a merchant, and with the business ticking over so profitably in someone else's hands he had the money to pursue whatever life he wanted. 'At this time I knew there was a general election coming on and at Hull the conversation often turned to politics and rooted me to ambition.'[1]

Eighteenth-century Elections and Parliament

Standing for parliament in eighteenth-century Britain was expensive. MPs were not paid, so politicians generally came from the wealthy landed class. Elections created more expense: firstly, to pay for any leaflets and canvassers to help get elected, and secondly because electors expected to be paid for voting. The electorate was only a small section of the male population, but they each had two votes, and expected to receive two pounds for one vote, or four pounds for two. If they lived outside their constituency they wanted travel expenses for coming home to vote too.

From ancient times, each town and each county sent two members to the House of Commons. The eighty members who represented the forty counties were considered the most prestigious MPs, and were generally allowed to speak first in debates. The town franchise was in need of reform; many modern towns and cities such as Manchester had no representation, whilst ancient ones that were virtually unpopulated still sent two MPs. This led to a system of pocket boroughs (where the voters were all in the 'pocket' of one landowner) and rotten boroughs (where the town population had become so reduced that the seat was basically in the hands of a local peer). The most infamous rotten boroughs were Old Sarum (which had a population of six people), and Dunwich (a coastal town abandoned when most of its buildings were flooded). But there were scores of them across the country.

Wilberforce could have found a patron and settled for a pocket borough, but he wanted to speak and vote with independence once in parliament. He decided to stand for his home town of Hull.

He spent much of the winter of 1779–80, his final year at Cambridge, at the public gallery of the House of Commons in London, following the parliamentary procedures and picking up an understanding of the place. He was joined in this by another 20-year-old man, also finishing Cambridge and planning on a political career. William Pitt was the son of a previous Prime Minister, Lord Chatham, and from an early age had determined to follow in his father's footsteps. He had been far more studious than Wilberforce at Cambridge, so the two had rarely met. Now they became close friends as they watched debates together, discussed politics, and plotted how each might get elected to the House. Wilberforce had few fixed views on political subjects, and quickly came to agree with Pitt on most issues.

Only men aged twenty-one or over could stand for election, but the timing proved perfect for Wilberforce. On his twenty-first birthday, 24 August 1780, he held an open party for all the voters of Hull, complete with free beer and a huge spit-roasted pig. One week later a general election was called. As a local boy, from one of Hull's leading families, someone universally popular on the social scene, a good speaker and with plenty of money to pay for votes, the Wilberforce campaign was unstoppable.

At one hustings someone threw a stone at him, causing a local butcher called Johnny Bell to offer to kill the culprit. Wilberforce talked Bell down from murder to merely frightening him. But this, along with riots and bribery, was standard practice for eighteenth-century elections. Wilberforce was duly voted MP for Hull, winning the same number of votes as his two opponents combined, and supplanting local MP David Hartley. 'The election cost me 8 or 9,000 £ – great riot – D. Hartley and Sir G. Savilles lodgings broke open in the night and they escaping over the roof'.[2]

London Life

In London Wilberforce lost no time becoming a man about town. He joined five of the exclusive gentlemen's clubs around Pall Mall, and started mingling with the very highest members of society.

High Society

I was at once immersed in politics and fashion. The very first time I went to Boodle's I won twenty-five guineas of the Duke of Norfolk. I belonged at this time to five clubs . . . Miles and Evans's, Brookes's, Boodle's, White's, Goostree's. The first time I was at Brookes's, scarcely knowing any one, I joined from mere shyness in play at the Faro table, where George Selwyn kept bank. A friend who knew my inexperience, and regarded me as a victim decked out for sacrifice, called to me, 'What, Wilberforce, is that you?' Selwyn quite resented the interference, and turning to him, said in his most expressive tone, 'O sir, don't interrupt Mr Wilberforce, he could not be better employed.' Nothing could be more luxurious than the style of these clubs. Fox, Sheridan, Fitzpatrick, and all your leading men, frequented them, and associated upon the easiest terms; you chatted, played at cards, or gambled as you pleased.[3]

With his beautiful singing voice, his talent for sparkling conversation (especially foining – verbal fencing over the meaning of words and phrases), and a newly found talent for doing impressions, he became popular everywhere. Even the young Prince of Wales, the future George IV and leader of the London social scene, became a fan: 'Wilberforce, we must have you again, the Prince says he will come at any time to hear you sing.'[4]

Talented Impressionist

Lord Camden noticed me particularly, and treated me with great kindness. Amongst other things, he cured me of the dangerous art of mimicry. When invited by my friends to witness my powers of imitation, he at once refused, saying slightingly for me to hear it, 'It is but a vulgar accomplishment.' 'Yes, but it is not imitating the mere manner; Wilberforce says the very thing Lord North would say.' 'Oh,' was his reply, 'every one does that.'[5]

Having given up mimicry, he also quickly stopped gambling. He lost £100 a night a few times, but it was the sight of seeing others less affluent than himself lose £600 and become financially ruined that took away his pleasure in the pastime.

In politics Wilberforce took up a seat with Pitt and others on the opposite side of the chamber to the current government. Lord North was the Prime Minister, unpopular in the country as the PM who had recently lost the American Revolutionary War. But Lord North remained more popular with the King than Charles Fox, who was leader of the Whig faction in parliament and close friends with the Prince of Wales.

Pitt's Eloquence

The papers will have informed you how Mr William Pitt, second son of the late Lord Chatham, has distinguished himself; he comes out as his father did a ready-made orator, and I doubt not but that I shall one day or other see him the first man in the country. His famous speech, however, delivered the other night, did not convince me, and I staid in with the old fat fellow [Lord North]: by the way he grows every day fatter, so where he will end I know not.[6]

Though Wilberforce did not always vote with Pitt, he was quite enthralled by his friend. 'He [Pitt] was the wittiest man I ever knew, and what was quite peculiar to himself, had at all times his wit under entire control.'[7] Due to his wealth, and his Wimbledon villa, Wilberforce would often entertain Pitt and other young political friends. '4th [April 1783]. Delicious day, – lounged morning at Wimbledon with friends, foining at night, and run about garden for an hour or two.'[8]

He did retain some occasional religious leanings. 'Sunday, July 6th [1783]. Wimbledon. Persuaded Pitt and Pepper to church.'[9] His diary for March 1783 also makes first mention of the poor quality of his eyesight, a problem which would gradually grow worse and plague him for the rest of his life, making it hard for him later on to read, study and write.

Visit to France

In summer 1783 Wilberforce, Pitt and a third friend Edward Eliot decided to visit France together. Each thought the other would bring letters of introduction for meeting French friends, so they ended up with only one contact across the Channel.

Botched Introductions

From Calais we made directly for Rheims, and the day after our arrival dressed ourselves unusually well, and proceeded to the house of a Mons. Coustier to present, with not a little awe, our only letters of recommendation. It was with some surprise that we found Mons. Coustier behind a counter distributing figs and raisins.[10]

Rather than being a local aristocrat, Mons. Coustier turned out to be a humble shopkeeper. With no contacts, and not much French between them, the three ended up renting a small room in a tavern, where their strange behaviour aroused the suspicions of the local policeman, and from him the local church leader.

Under Suspicion from the Church

One morning when the intendant of police brought me his daily report, he informed me, there are three Englishmen here of very suspicious character. They are in a wretched lodging, they have no attendance, yet their courier says, that they are 'grands seigneurs,' and that one of them is son of the great Chatham; but it is impossible, they must be 'des intrigants.'[11]

Once he established they were not spies, the helpful Abbe De Lageard introduced them to the local Archbishop, who in turn got Pitt some wine (he'd complained they'd been in France a week and still not had a drop to drink), and introduced them to wider society.

Their visit now picked up. In Paris they met King Louis XVI, became guests at the royal court, and became friends with Queen Marie Antoinette (who often playfully asked if they had heard anything from their friend the grocer). They also met Benjamin Franklin, ambassador to France for the newly independent United States of America.

The Prime Minister's Best Friend

The trio returned to England on 24 October 1783. Wilberforce resumed a life of regular attendance at parliament, Goostree's Club, and having friends to stay at Wimbledon.

Pitt had more pressing matters to attend to. Lord North had finally resigned in 1782. Since then there had been three Prime Ministers, none of whom lasted long. In December 1783, in desperation from not wanting to have Charles Fox as PM, the King appointed William Pitt as Prime Minister of Great Britain. He was 24 years old, and Wilberforce was his closest friend.

Pitt had the support of the King, but he didn't have the support of parliament. Fox led a no confidence motion against his government that was passed by 39 votes. Normally a PM who lost a no confidence motion would resign, but Pitt knew he retained the support of the King, so he stayed in office. For week after week the opposition passed resolutions opposing him, but Pitt refused to go. He counted on a new force that was now entering politics. Petitions supporting the King and the PM started to arrive at parliament from towns and cities across Britain. The advent of newspapers meant for the first time people could follow parliamentary procedures and receive news just a day after they happened. People were stirred up into believing they needed to support an honest King and PM, against a corrupt and licentious opposition led by Fox. And as the petitions came in, more MPs took note of public opinion, and sided with Pitt.

After two months of this, in March 1784 Pitt finally had a majority in the Commons. He then immediately called a general election, banking on the trend to continue in his favour, and that the newly returned parliament would provide him with substantial backing.

Member for Yorkshire

Wilberforce had supported Pitt throughout this time, and the two were close confidants, but now Wilberforce decided to make a radical bid of his own.

An Ambitious Idea

I had formed within my own heart the project of standing for the county. To any one besides myself I was aware that it must appear so mad a scheme, that I never mentioned it to Mr Pitt, or any of my political connexions. It was undoubtedly a bold idea, but I was then very ambitious.[12]

To represent a county seat gave a politician far more prominence in parliament. And Yorkshire was not just any county seat; it was the largest county in the nation, making it one of the most prestigious. Fox himself often commented, 'Yorkshire and Middlesex between them make all England.'[13]

But to represent a county was also incredibly expensive; it cost far more money than even Wilberforce had at his disposal. Full county elections were rarely held due to the expense of paying so many voters. Instead smaller groups would listen to candidates at hustings across the county, and simply send to parliament the two they thought were the most popular. Candidates could contest these decisions if they wanted, but would then have to foot the bill for a very expensive election.

Wilberforce knew all this as he travelled to York in March 1784 for a meeting where the voters were considering sending a loyal address and petition to the King. There were large numbers of speakers assembled for and against, and it must have been humbling for Wilberforce to find that he was only scheduled to speak at 4 p.m., at an all-day open-air meeting that began at 10 a.m. By the time he started speaking it was raining, and many thought the frail young man who got up would not be heard over the weather. In fact he produced the best and the clearest heard speech of the day. One observer said, 'I saw what seemed a mere shrimp mount upon the table; but, as I listened, he grew, and grew, until the shrimp became a whale.'[14]

The four thousand people assembled were transfixed by his words. An hour into his speech a messenger on horseback galloped up with a personal letter from Pitt, announcing the immediate dissolution of parliament and fresh elections. Wilberforce relayed this to the crowd, and such was the effect his speech had made that many started shouting, 'We'll have this man for our county member!'[15] It was a speech that changed his life.

Two weeks later, after a whirlwind of campaigning and hustings, his Yorkshire opponents conceded defeat.

Wilberforce wrote to Eliot excitedly, 'I am or at least shall be tomorrow (our enemies having this evening declared their intentions of declining a Poll) Knight of the Shire for the County of York.'[16]

It was an incredible victory, and another huge leap forward for Wilberforce. The whole election was a huge victory and vindication for Pitt, who now had a triple figure parliamentary majority, and was himself returned for the constituency he prized above all others, Cambridge University (at his first election he had taken a pocket borough). He wrote from Downing Street to his friend, 'My dear Wilberforce, I can never enough congratulate you on such glorious success.'[17]

Wilberforce truly was a glorious success in many areas of life. Aged twenty-five he had already achieved all he might have dreamed of just a few years previously: a young man of independent fortune, MP for Yorkshire, best friends with the Prime Minister, a talented speaker, and universally popular in the most prestigious London clubs. He owned a villa in Wimbledon, and in 1782 took seven years' rental on a retreat property called Rayrigg near Windermere, so he could holiday in the Lake District. What more could a young man dream of? William Wilberforce had truly arrived.

A Man of Consequence

Key Learning Points

Spiritual Formation

Offer hospitality. Be generous with your home in providing a place for others to stay.

Don't gamble. If nothing else, think of those you are taking money from. Many can ill afford to lose.

Discerning Vision

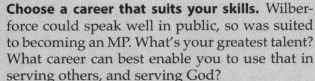

Choose a career that suits your skills. Wilberforce could speak well in public, so was suited to becoming an MP. What's your greatest talent? What career can best enable you to use that in serving others, and serving God?

Key moments can change everything. Wilberforce's Yorkshire speech changed his life. How can you prepare for the key moments that might change yours? What gifts should you sharpen so they are ready for those moments?

Ambition can take you places. Ambition can be destructive when it's purely selfish, but can be positive when it's ambition for a cause. Wilberforce began with ambition for himself, but grew to have greater ambitions.

Leadership Skills

Who you know is important. In Rheims, in Paris and in London, who Wilberforce knew opened up or limited his worlds. Who do you know, and who do you want to get to know?

Good communication is vital. Do all you can to develop as a public speaker. It will enhance your leadership.

The Great Change: 1784–1787

On becoming MP for Yorkshire Wilberforce went on a European tour with a friend. Whilst there, a discussion about Christianity led to a reappraisal of his life, and a three-year journey of rediscovery towards his childhood faith.

Visit to Europe

After the 1784 election Wilberforce was invited to accompany his mother and sister Sarah on a tour to the Alps. The trip would include long carriage journeys through France and Switzerland. Wilberforce insisted he bring along a companion for male conversation. He could then chat with his family over dinner and in the evenings, but talk with his friend during the journeys in the days.

On a visit back to Yorkshire he met Isaac Milner, younger brother of his old school master Joseph Milner, and an old childhood friend. He asked Milner to be his European companion on the spot. Milner was an ordained Church of England vicar, but he seemed a jolly enough fellow who didn't have a problem joining in with card games, so Wilberforce thought he would be great company.

Isaac Milner

He [Milner] was free from every taint of vice but not more attentive than others to religion; he appeared in all respects like an ordinary man of the world, mixing like myself in all companies, and joining as readily as others in the prevalent Sunday parties. Indeed, when I engaged him as a companion in my tour, I knew not that he had any deeper principles. The first time I discovered it, was at the public table at Scarborough. The conversation turned on Mr Stillingfleet [an evangelical rector]; and I spoke of him as a good man, but one who carried things too far. – 'Not a bit too far,' said Milner; and to this opinion he adhered, when we renewed the conversation in the evening on the sands. This declaration greatly surprised me; and it was agreed that at some future time we would talk the matter over.[1]

Wilberforce was surprised Milner had such a high opinion of an evangelical clergyman, and pressed him on it as they began their journey through France. After his childhood Methodism, Wilberforce had come to the opinion that all evangelicals were either hypocrites or deluded enthusiasts, and that being a Christian was simply about following a certain level of morality. They began a discussion, but Wilberforce's background in foining and parliamentary arguments made him treat the subject as a debating competition rather than a serious conversation. 'I am no match for you, Wilberforce, in this running fire, but if you really wish to discuss these subjects seriously, I will gladly enter on them with you.'[2] This changed the discussion to something more serious.

After only a short time in the Alps, Wilberforce was summoned back to parliament by Pitt for a series of debates on parliamentary reform where the PM wanted his support. Wilberforce suggested to Milner they discuss Philip Doddridge's book *The Rise and Progress of Religion in the Soul* as they travelled to London. Milner agreed: 'It is one of the best books ever written, let us take it with us and read it on our journey.'[3]

They made it back to London, but the reform debates were lost, so Wilberforce and Milner again set out for the Alps, to rejoin Mrs and Miss Wilberforce in Switzerland. By now it was early 1785, and the religious discussion for both had become so serious they were studying the New Testament in Greek, to check if Doddridge and the evangelicals were right about what they claimed to be the essence of real Christianity. By the time they reached Switzerland both were so engrossed in their studies and discussions the ladies complained they saw no more of them now they were all together in Geneva compared to when the men were in London.

Studying the Bible

In the course of this journey Milner and I resumed the subject of religion, and my former convictions were confirmed and deepened. We read parts of the New Testament together, when I pressed on him my various doubts, objections, and difficulties. The final result of our discussions was a settled conviction in my mind, not only of the truth of Christianity, but also of the Scriptural basis of the leading doctrines.[4]

Spiritual Beginnings

It had been a series of geographical and theological journeys lasting nearly twelve months, but by summer 1785 Wilberforce had examined the Bible and decided the evangelical doctrine of salvation in Jesus was true. But how should that truth affect his conduct?

Milner's Influence

By degrees I imbibed his [Milner's] sentiments, though I must confess with shame, that they long remained merely as opinions assented to by my understanding, but not influencing my heart. My interest in them certainly increased, and at length I began to be impressed with a sense of their importance. Milner, though full of levity on all other subjects, never spoke on this but with the utmost seriousness, and all he said, tended to increase my attention to religion.[5]

The Great Change was upon him. He was returning to the faith he had briefly experienced in his childhood. Slowly he began to respond to God's promptings. Back in London in autumn 1785, feeling convicted of sin but with no sense of God's forgiveness, he began to pray so he could find peace.

Diary Entries

October 25th. Began three or four days ago to get up very early. In the solitude and self-conversation of the morning had thoughts, which I trust will come to something.

November 27th. My heart is so hard, my blindness so great, that I cannot get a due hatred of sin, though I see I am all corrupt, and blinded to the perception of spiritual things.

November 29th. I bless God I enjoyed comfort in prayer this evening.

November 30th. I thought seriously this evening of going to converse with Mr [John] Newton – waked in the night – obliged to compel myself to think of God.

December 2nd. Resolved again about Mr Newton. It may do good; he will pray for me; his experience may enable him to direct me to new grounds of humiliation, and it is that only which I can perceive God's Spirit employ to any effect. It can do no harm, for that is a scandalous objection which keeps occurring to me, that if ever my sentiments change, I shall be ashamed of having done it: it can only humble me, and, whatever is the right way, if truth be right I ought to be humbled – but, sentiments change![6]

Wilberforce had fond memories of Newton from his childhood. Newton was now vicar at St Mary Woolnoth in London, close at hand and able to give spiritual advice. But to visit Newton publicly would be to risk his position in society; it would risk the ridicule and reputation of being a Methodist, the very thing his mother had rescued him from fifteen years earlier.

Conversations with Pitt

Before finding the courage to visit Newton, Wilberforce shared his new-found feelings on religion with his closest friend.

Letter to Pitt

I wrote to Mr Pitt, frankly communicating to him the great change that had taken place in my views, and the effects which this change would probably produce upon my public conduct. I told him, that although I should ever feel the greatest regard and affection for him, and had every reason to believe that I should in general be able to support his measures, I could no longer act as a party man.[7]

He also told Pitt he was considering quitting politics, at least for a time, so he could discern what life God was now calling him to lead. Pitt wrote back a letter full of concern, requesting the chance to talk things through in person, and asking how long he planned to be away from politics.

When they met, 'He tried to reason me out of my convictions, but soon found himself unable to combat their correctness, if Christianity were true. The fact is, he was so absorbed in politics, that he had never given himself time for due reflection of religion.'[8] Pitt was absorbed with politics, and didn't want to lose his closest friend from the world they now shared – that was how Wilberforce interpreted his advice.

Conversations with Newton

Wilberforce finally overcame his fears and approached Newton for a meeting on 4th December 1785.

Letter to Newton

Sir,
There is no need of apology for intruding on you, when the errand is religion. I wish to have some serious conversation with you, and will take the liberty of calling on you for that purpose, in half an hour; when, if you cannot receive me, you will have the goodness to let me have a letter put into my hands at the door, naming a time and place for our meeting, the earlier the more agreeable to me. I have had ten thousand doubts within myself, whether or not I should discover myself to you; but every argument against doing it has its foundation in pride. I am sure you will hold yourself bound to let no one living know of this application, or of my visit, till I release you from the obligation.

P.S. Remember that I must be secret, and that the gallery of the House is now so universally attended, that the face of a member of parliament is pretty well known.[9]

Finding Newton busy, they arranged to meet at St Mary Woolnoth three days later.

Meeting Again

After walking about the Square once or twice before I could persuade myself, I called upon old Newton – was much affected in conversing with him – something very pleasing and unaffected in him. He told me he always had entertained hopes and confidence that God would some time bring me to Him.[10]

Wilberforce went believing that Newton would advise him to leave politics, break off with the friends he currently associated with in London, and possibly consider a career in the church. He had enough self-awareness to know his greatest gifts were in public speaking. Should he not use his voice and his talent as a preacher? But Newton gave quite different advice. 'Mr Newton, in the interviews I had with him, advised me to avoid at present making many religious acquaintances, and to keep up my connection with Pitt, and to continue in Parliament.'[11]

The one new religious acquaintance Newton did encourage was with the Thornton family – the family of his Aunt Hannah. Uncle William had died, but Aunt Hannah now lived with her half-brother John Thornton in Clapham. Wilberforce renewed his relationship with his aunt, and started visiting the Thorntons regularly. John Thornton agreed with Newton's advice: 'You cannot be too wary in forming connexions. The fewer new friends, perhaps, the better. I shall at any time be glad to see you here, and can quarter you, and let you be as retired as possible.'[12]

So Wilberforce continued to associate with Newton and the Thorntons over the Christmas and New Year period of 1785/86. Through their prayers and encouragement, he started to be comfortable with his new-found faith. '12th [January]. Newton staid – Thornton Astell surprised us together on the common in the evening. Expect to hear myself now universally given out to be a Methodist: may God grant it may be said with truth.'[13]

Reaction of Society

Society did not immediately pillory him as a Methodist, but he still worried about what others would think of his conversion, and also about what he now felt unable to do as a practising Christian. He continued to be a regular social visitor at Downing Street, and to associate with Pitt and his other political friends, but he resigned his membership at the five London clubs, feeling their dedication to drinking, gambling and prestige was incompatible with his new way of life.

Most of all he dreaded the reaction of his mother, who had rescued him from Methodism all those years ago. Turning to Christianity was often described as 'growing serious' by society, since those who found God often turned their backs on all pleasure, and became serious, even gloomy; never laughing, and only talking about serious subjects. Wilberforce strove against this, and partly on Pitt's and Newton's advice resolved to become a joyful Christian. So when he finally caught up with his mother in Yorkshire in summer 1786 he made sure that joy was a key part of her impression of him. To his family, rather than becoming serious, his conversion made him happier and more caring. A friend of his mother's remarked during the visit, 'If this is madness, I hope that he will bite us all.'[14]

He did change something of his social conduct though. As someone who had previously loved *foining*, he now became frustrated with the pastime. In society his greatest temptations were foolish talk, and eating too much at the opulent dinner tables of the late eighteenth century. That autumn he created a set of rules to regulate his conduct when going out for dinner.

Rules for Conduct

No dessert, no tastings, one thing in first, one in second course. Simplicity. In quantity moderate . . . Never more than six glasses of wine; my common allowance two or three . . . To be in bed always if possible by eleven and to be up by six o'clock. In general to reform in accordance with my so often repeated resolutions . . . I will every night note down whether have been so or not.[15]

He continued making rules to guide his conduct throughout his life, and advised others to do the same. But he insisted individual Christians create rules for themselves rather than impose them on others, and that the Bible was the best source for advice on how to act in each situation.

Advice to a Friend

I conceive no rule can be prescribed of universal application and use – none that will solve to every one the several cases which occur in life, under the very different circumstances of different men; and yet, unless we lay down for ourselves beforehand some determinate principle of action, when the time for decision comes we shall be at a loss how to proceed, and, judging hastily and under an improper bias, our conclusion

> will most likely be erroneous. What then is to be done? What but that every one read his Bible with simplicity of heart, that he there observe the temper and conduct our Saviour prescribes to His disciples, and then, looking into and weighing the particulars of his own state, discover how he may best acquire the one and practise the other. Where any thing is directly contrary to the laws of God there we ought to resist as stubbornly as possible.[16]

His new faith also led to a change in living circumstances. Deciding as a single man he couldn't justify the expense of keeping a large country residence, he sold Lauriston House in Wimbledon, and bought a house opposite parliament on Old Palace Yard. On top of money this also saved time; he was now only ever a short walk away from his main place of work. He started to attend the Commons far more frequently than most other MPs, and was nicknamed the 'nightingale of the house', partly due to his beautiful voice, but also due to being ever present at the late night debates.

Should he ever need a country retreat outside the centre of town, John Thornton offered him uninterrupted use of rooms at the Thornton's Clapham estate, without any obligation of their having to spend time together: 'Young men and old have different habits, and I shall leave you therefore to keep your own hours, and take care that you are not interrupted.'[17]

Proclamation Society

By now Wilberforce was sufficiently confident to wonder how he could use his political position to further the

Kingdom of God. Being concerned about the vice and corruption throughout society, he saw that previous monarchs had issued proclamations when they came to the throne, exhorting their subjects to become more virtuous. By 1787 George III had been King for twenty-seven years, but he was a man of strict morals known to be angered by the licentious behaviour of his children. Wilberforce reasoned he could be persuaded to issue a new proclamation against vice. And to give the proclamation more teeth he set up a Proclamation Society to give effect to its rulings.

He was supported by Beilby Porteus, the Bishop of London. Porteus agreed to the creation of a Society, and suggested enlisting senior bishops, lords and politicians into its ranks before it went public. With them on board it would have enough momentum to continue to gain membership and affect the grassroots.

Society Membership and Objects

I mean the society to publish a list of its members, and an account of its institution, when sufficiently numerous and respectable. It should consist of persons of consequence in every line of life, the professions, members of both Houses, merchants in the city, aldermen, &c. I have no doubt of the Duke of Montagu's accepting the office of president, and have reason to believe that the Archbishop of Canterbury will give us his name, in which case the rest of the bench will follow his example. The objects to which the committee will direct their attention are the offences specified in the Proclamation, – profanation of the sabbath, swearing, drunkenness, licentious publications, unlicensed places of public amusement, the regulation of licensed places, &c.[18]

When the royal proclamation was issued on 1 June 1787, the Proclamation Society's membership included the Archbishops of Canterbury and York, 17 other bishops, 6 dukes, 1 marquess, 10 lords, and the Prime Minister.

Proclamation Society Text

We, the undersigned, truly sensible of His Majesty's tender and watchful concern for the happiness of his people, manifested in his late royal Proclamation, and being convinced of the necessity, in the present juncture, of our attending to His Majesty's call on all his faithful subjects to check the rapid progress of impiety and licentiousness, to promote a spirit of decency and good order, and enforce a stricter execution of the laws against vice and immorality, do agree to form ourselves into a Society, for the purpose of carrying His Majesty's gracious recommendation into effect.[19]

Role in Society

Continuing his active attendance at parliament, and his friendships with senior ministers, new opportunities of service opened up. Through his intervention the first chaplains were sent to the new penal colony of Australia, to attend to the spiritual needs of the transported convicts. Newton encouraged him to continue serving God in his parliamentary role.

Advice of John Newton

I have learned to be content, even in a favourable situation. You likewise, Sir, are in your post, and yours is a post of honour. Many, perhaps, who view you from a distance, envy you, and would be glad to change places with you: I love and respect you, but I do not envy you: perhaps you have less time at your own disposal, and meet with more things in your path, which do not accord with your inclination, than myself. But if you are, upon the whole, where and what the Lord would have you to be, this thought reconciles you to the unavoidables which are connected with your situation; and I hope great usefulness to the public, and to the church of God, will be your present reward.

To you, as the instrument, we owe the pleasing prospect of an opening for the propagation of the Gospel in the Southern Hemisphere. Who can tell what important consequences may depend upon Mr Johnson's going to New Holland [first chaplain sent to New South Wales]?[20]

By autumn 1787 he had reconciled his spiritual life with his political vocation, and embraced his role to be a voice for God in parliament. First the Proclamation Society, then sending missionaries to British colonies. And now a new task he would dedicate the remainder of his life towards opened up before him. On 28 October 1787 he wrote in his journal, 'God Almighty has set before me two great objects, the suppression of the slave trade and the reformation of manners.'[21]

The Great Change

Key Learning Points

Spiritual Formation

Talk with people about God. The conversations Wilberforce had with Milner changed his life.

Admire beauty in creation. The majestic scenery of the Alps helped Wilberforce in his worship of God as Creator.

Study the Bible. Learn what it teaches about God and humanity. This study became the basis for Wilberforce's faith.

Respond to God's promptings. Wilberforce prayed, meditated, started a journal and went to visit John Newton for advice. Don't be passive but active in spiritual formation.

Don't be embarrassed about Jesus. Don't allow peer pressure to stop you from doing God's will.

Plan for your conduct. Creating rules or guidelines for how you will behave in different situations can help you stand firm for God when the time comes.

Be joyful. Believing in Jesus may make you more serious on some matters, but Christians are to be joyful people.

Don't cut off your friends. Some things are to be given up as we follow God, but friendships are not one of them.

Economize with time and money. Save the expense to spend on things that truly matter.

Discerning Vision

 Start serving God. We are called to serve him from the first moment we are called into relationship with him. Wilberforce began by sending missionaries to Australia and forming the Proclamation Society. What are you able to do?

Leadership Skills

 Work with those in power. Where you can, work through the existing system rather than creating something else. Wilberforce invited bishops, lords and politicians to the Proclamation Society to give it extra weight.

Work with a team. You can't do everything on your own. Join with others in societies or other endeavours to be able to achieve more.

The Trade in Flesh and Blood: 1787–1789

The British were the leading slave traders of the day, transporting around 40,000 people per year from the coasts of West Africa to the plantations of North America and the Caribbean. It was this slave trade, and the powerful commercial interests that lay behind it, that Wilberforce now dedicated his life to fighting.

'The first years that I was in parliament I did nothing – nothing I mean to any good purpose; my own distinction was my darling object.'[1] But now Wilberforce had found causes to live for. By 'reformation of manners' he meant a wholesale change in the morality of the nation, and he had made a beginning with the Proclamation Society. He would come back to this cause in various ways over the years. But his main time would now be taken up with the abolition of the slave trade.

Joining the Fighters

Prior to Wilberforce's 1787 commitment to the abolition movement, there were many other individuals already involved in the fight. The Quakers were the most prominent organisation who condemned slavery. They had raised petitions and tried to mobilize public opinion, but they were seen as a fringe organisation by most of the country.

An Anglican vicar called James Ramsey had worked in the West Indies, seen the brutal conditions and treatment the slaves suffered under, and returned to the UK determined to fight against slavery. He provided information and statistics on the nature of West Indian slavery, and in an indication of what the pro-slavery lobby would do, he became vilified and nearly bankrupted because of his work.

The Triangular Atlantic Slave Trade

The transatlantic slave trade had been carried on for almost as long as transatlantic navigation had been taking place. Christopher Columbus first crossed the Atlantic in 1492, and by 1502 there were the beginnings of a regular slave trade taking slaves from Africa to the New World.

There were numerous slave trade routes across the Atlantic. The Portuguese took Africans from the coasts of Angola and transported them to Brazil, and the French from West Africa to their own colonies in the West Indies. The British captured slaves from West Africa and took them to North America and the Caribbean, in what became known as The Triangular Trade. Ships left Britain loaded with guns, cloth, trinkets and other materials to barter with African chiefs for slaves. They left Africa with ships loaded with captured slaves to cross the Atlantic on what became known as the Middle Passage. They then sold the slaves to the plantation owners in the West Indies, and brought their ships home to Britain laden with cotton, sugar, rum and the other crops cultivated by slaves.

A slave voyage therefore took a triangular route: from Britain to Africa to the West Indies and back to Britain. It took several months to complete, and a successful slave captain was able to make profits on all three legs of the voyage.

Granville Sharp

The leading British abolitionist was Granville Sharp, an eccentric musician and self-taught lawyer who in 1765 found a beaten black man dying on the streets of London. Jonathan Strong was a West Indian slave brought to England by his master, beaten up and left for dead. Sharp played the Good Samaritan role, getting Strong medical treatment that saved his life, and then arranging a job for him when he recovered. Two years later Strong's former master found him, saw he was in good health, and tried to sell him to a group of planters who would take him back to slavery in Jamaica. Sharp found out about the sale, and had Strong freed by threatening to take the case to court.

In 1772 Sharp defended a similar case for James Somerset. This time the case went to trial, with Sharp arguing that English law did not recognize slavery, and that Somerset could not therefore be sold to someone else whilst on English soil, even by his legal owner in the West Indies. The case was upheld and Somerset freed, leading the poet William Cowper to write:

Slaves cannot breath in England; if their lungs
Receive our air, that moment they are free.

Lord Mansfield was the judge in the Somerset case, and pointed out 'The judgement . . . went no further than to determine the Master had no right to compel the slave to go into a foreign country.'[2] But Cowper and most of the country took it to mean that slavery had been outlawed in Britain. It seemed a first victory for the abolitionists.

But a subsequent case showed just how far there still was to go. In 1783 Lord Mansfield presided over a case involving the *Zong*, a slave ship that had sailed from Africa to Jamaica in 1781. Due to navigation errors and an inexperienced crew they arrived in the West Indies later than planned and running low on drinking water. If slaves died on board due to lack of water, or arrived in the West Indies so ill and dehydrated they would not fetch a good price, the owners would make nothing from the voyage. But the crew realized if they threw slaves into the sea because they were running low on water, they could claim on their insurance for loss of cargo. From 442 slaves on board, 92 died of illness during the Middle Passage, 208 were sold when the ship finally reached Jamaica, but 142 were thrown overboard and drowned. The owners put in an insurance claim for the 142 who had been murdered; the insurance company refused to pay out. In court Lord Mansfield gave judgement in favour of the slave ship, and against the insurance company: 'the Blacks were property . . . [it was] . . . just as if horses were killed'.[3]

The case showed why abolition would prove so difficult to achieve. Outside of Britain, slaves were regarded as property, to be disposed of as the owner pleased. Kidnapping free people and forcing them into slavery was illegal in British law, but the British slave traders were not doing the kidnapping. African slave traders were the ones kidnapping African men, women and children, marching them to the coast, and selling them to the white slave traders. British slave traders in the eyes of British law were not doing anything illegal, they were merely buying and selling property. The slave trade, according to one British MP, 'was not an amiable trade, but neither was the trade of a butcher an amiable trade, and yet a mutton chop was, nevertheless, a very good thing'.[4]

Olaudah Equiano

Equiano was kidnapped into slavery from modern day Nigeria when a young boy. He spent many years working for various masters in the West Indies, managed to buy his own freedom, and eventually settled in England where he wrote a book of his experiences, and became a leading black abolitionist spokesman.

[On his kidnapping] *One day, when all our people were gone out to their works as usual, and only I and my dear sister were left to mind the house, two men and a woman got over our walls, and in a moment seized us both; and, without giving us time to cry out, or make resistance, they stopped our mouths, and ran off with us into the nearest wood. Here they tied our hands, and continued to carry us as far as they could, till night came on, when we reached a small house, where the robbers halted for refreshment, and spent the night.*[5]

[On first meeting white slave traders] *I feared I should be put to death, the white people looked and acted, as I thought, in so savage a manner; for I had never seen among any people such instances of brutal cruelty; and this not only shewn towards us blacks, but also to some of the whites themselves.*[6]

[On the Middle Passage] *The closeness of the place, and the heat of the climate, added to the number in the ship, which was so crowded that each had scarcely room to turn himself, almost suffocated us. This produced copious perspirations, so that the air soon became unfit for respiration, from a variety of loathsome smells, and brought on a sickness among the slaves, of which many died, thus falling victims to the improvident avarice, as I may call it, of their purchasers. This wretched situation was again aggravated by the galling of the chains, now become insupportable; and the filth of the necessary tubs, into which the children often fell, and were almost suffocated. The shrieks of the women, and the groans of the dying, rendered the whole a scene of horror almost inconceivable.*[7]

[On the West Indies] *It was almost a constant practice with our clerks, and other whites, to commit violent depredations on the chastity of the female slaves . . . I have even known them gratify their brutal passion with females not ten years old . . . And yet in Montserrat I have seen a negro-man staked to the ground, and cut most shockingly, and then his ears cut off bit by bit, because he had been connected with a white woman who was a common prostitute.*[8]

Thomas Clarkson

The other main abolitionist Wilberforce came into contact with was a 27-year-old deacon called Thomas Clarkson, destined to be one of his greatest partners. Whilst studying at Cambridge Clarkson entered an annual university essay competition. The subject that year was *Is it lawful to enslave the unconsenting?* Clarkson threw himself into studying the subject of slavery, and wrote a masterful essay that won him the coveted first prize. When he finished Cambridge, he rode to London in June 1785 to take up a position as a clergyman and, en route, had what he later described as a spiritual experience.

Clarkson's Commitment to Abolition

I became at times very seriously affected while upon the road. I stopped my horse occasionally, and dismounted and walked. I frequently tried to persuade myself in these intervals that the contents of my Essay could not be true. The more however I reflected upon them, or rather upon the authorities on which they were founded, the more I gave them credit . . .

Coming in sight of Wades Mill in Hertfordshire, I sat down disconsolate on the turf by the roadside and held my horse. Here a thought came into my mind, that if the contents of the Essay were true, it was time some person should see these calamities to their end.

Wilberforce and Abolition

Wilberforce had got to know Ramsey, Sharp, Equiano, Clarkson and many others by autumn 1787. His own commitment to abolition had been a journey of many years, and one that overlapped with his conversion.

His family later claimed that as a 14-year-old boy Wilberforce wrote to a Hull newspaper condemning the slave trade. No record of this letter exists. The first time we know he mentioned the subject was the 1780 election campaign at Hull, when he defeated David Hartley. Ironically, Hartley was one of the few MPs to have raised the issue in parliament, and Wilberforce had taken his seat. 'I expressed my hope to him that the time would come when

I should be able to do something on behalf of slaves.'[10] Perhaps he felt a debt to look further into the issue, and did some reading around it during his first years in parliament.

He undoubtedly heard of the slave trade from John Newton when he first met him as a young boy during his Wimbledon years. And since his conversion and renewed friendship with Newton, it's quite possible he had discussed the trade with the slave trader turned vicar. Perhaps Newton encouraged Wilberforce that speaking out in parliament on the issue of slavery was one of the ways he could be of great use to the public as a Christian statesman.

In 1783 Wilberforce met James Ramsey, and heard firsthand accounts of the brutality of slavery in the West Indies. From here on he started paying more serious attention to the issue, and spoke with a number of others about it. By 1786 the fledgling abolitionists had realized they needed a parliamentary champion for their cause, and having heard of his conversion were already looking to approach Wilberforce. One wrote to him, asking him to take on the leadership of a parliamentary campaign against the slave trade.

Thomas Clarkson also by now had heard that the famous MP for Yorkshire was interested in the issue, and paid Wilberforce a visit in early 1787 to present a copy of his prize-winning essay. Clarkson then arranged a formal dinner in March 1787 where Wilberforce was present, and was invited to lead the parliamentary campaign. 'He had no objection to bring forward the measure in Parliament, when he was better prepared for it, and provided no person more proper could be found.'[11]

Wilberforce was interested, but would not make a final decision until he had spoken with his closest political friend. His conversation with William Pitt on 12 May 1787 marked a turning point.

Wilberforce's Commitment to Abolition

In 1787 I was staying with Pitt at Holwood – one has often a local recollection of particular incidents – and I distinctly remember the very knoll upon which I was sitting, near Pitt and Grenville, when the former said to me, 'Wilberforce, why don't you give notice of a motion on the subject of the slave trade? You have already taken great pains to collect evidence, and are therefore fully entitled to the credit which doing so will ensure you. Do not lose time, or the ground may be occupied by another.'[12]

With the support of his friend and Prime Minister, Wilberforce finally felt able to take on the task of fighting against the slave trade in parliament.

The Beginnings

On 22 May 1787 Clarkson convened the inaugural meeting of the Society for Effecting the Abolition of the Slave Trade. There were 12 members present: 9 Quakers and 3 Anglicans, including Clarkson and Granville Sharp. Sharp was elected chairman, and Clarkson secretary and primary researcher for the group. Wilberforce wasn't present, but the group already knew he would be their parliamentary champion. Sharp wrote, 'Mr W. is to introduce the business to the House. The respectability of his position as member for the largest county, the great influence of his personal connexions, added to an amiable and unblemished character, secure every advantage to the cause.'[13] The Abolition movement had been born.

Right from the beginning the committee made a tactical choice to focus on the abolition of the slave trade, rather than the abolition of slavery itself. All of them abhorred slavery and ultimately wanted to see it outlawed. But they knew the chances of parliament passing a law that all slaves should be set free were slim. That would require plantation owners to give up their cherished 'property' by enabling slaves they had paid money for to go free.

Campaigning for a ban on the slave trade itself was a much more achievable goal. And they reasoned the abolition of the trade would in turn lead to improved conditions for slaves in the West Indies: planters would no longer work slaves to death if they couldn't buy replacements. In the words of Clarkson, abolishing the trade in slaves was 'laying the axe at the very root'[14] of the whole system of West Indian slavery. Abolition of the trade became the movement's aim, with eventual emancipation for existing slaves only far into the future as a goal.

Illness

Clarkson spent five months in summer and autumn 1787 visiting the port cities of Bristol and Liverpool, interviewing sailors and learning as much as he could about conditions on board slave ships, to give Wilberforce evidence for the coming parliamentary campaign. Wilberforce set about mastering this information for a debate in the Commons, but then disaster struck.

On 19 February 1788 he became severely ill. A problem with his digestive organs caused him to lose weight, and mystified his doctors. Rather than be able to fight in the Commons to ban the slave trade, he ended up fighting for his life. The doctors told him he had just two weeks to live. Sent to Bath to convalesce, he extracted a promise from Pitt to introduce the topic to the House, and to carry on the fight if he should die.

Wilberforce's Illness

As to the Slave question, I do not like to touch on it, it is so big a one it frightens me in my present weak state. Suffice it to say, and I know the pleasure it will afford you to hear it, that I trust matters are in very good train. *To you in strict confidence I will intrust*, that Pitt, with a warmth of principle and friendship that have made me love him better than I ever did before, has taken on himself the management of the business, and promises to do *all* for me if I desire it, that, if I were an efficient man, it would be proper for me to do myself.[15]

Later doctors have reasoned Wilberforce was suffering from ulcerative colitis. At the time they just knew that something was wrong with his stomach and his digestive system. Not knowing the full illness, they were at a loss on how to prescribe a cure. So they gave him one of the most unlikely cures imaginable to our age, but one that seemed to actually do the trick . . . they encouraged him to start taking opium.

For the rest of his life Wilberforce took four grains of opium every day. If he ever missed a dose he quickly became incapacitated through stomach and bowel troubles. But remarkably, unlike many other regular opium users, he never needed to increase his dosage due to addiction. Also remarkably, taking the drug so regularly seems not to have had any detrimental effect on the rest of his body, and actually kept his digestion problems at bay.

The Opening Salvos

With Wilberforce still severely ill but at least recovering, Pitt introduced the subject of the slave trade to parliament for the first time. Moving cautiously, rather than introducing a motion to ban the trade, Pitt asked that parliament sanction a full investigation into the nature of the trade. He and Wilberforce reasoned that an enquiry would expose the immorality and barbarity of the trade to MPs, and also force those in favour of the trade to declare themselves and their arguments publicly.

Pitt was unopposed when he asked for an enquiry, but that summer another parliamentary bill showed the opposition to come. William Dolben was one of the few MPs already committed to abolition. Having done some of his own research, he proposed a bill to reduce overcrowding and improve conditions during the Middle Passage. The bill was passed in July 1788 after stormy parliamentary sessions, and it revealed the key opponents of abolition to be the Liverpool MPs and the West Indian lobby groups, who argued that even this severely limited form of regulation would lead to anarchy in the Caribbean and bankruptcy to the economy.

Parliamentary Procedures

To become law an Act of Parliament had to go through several stages. The draft act, known as a bill, needed to be voted for by a majority on three separate occasions in the House of Commons, and also three separate times in the House of Lords. Each of these were called readings, i.e. first reading, second reading and third reading. Defeat on any reading meant the bill was killed off. Only when a bill had passed all three readings in both Houses would it be given Royal Assent, i.e. signed into law by the sovereign to become an Act of Parliament. Passing a bill banning the slave trade would not be the work of a moment, but would require a sustained campaign, and the support of a clear majority of MPs and lords.

Wilberforce had missed all the parliamentary sessions where Pitt's enquiry and Dolben's Middle Passage Bill were debated. But by summer 1788 and the parliamentary recess he was beginning to recover. He left Bath and went to his Lake District property of Rayrigg to convalesce in peace and quiet.

A Summer at Rayrigg

My general object, during my stay at this place, should be to guard against habits of idleness, luxury, selfishness, and forgetfulness of God, by interlacing as much as I can of reading, and meditation, and religious retirement, and self-examination. Let me constantly view myself in all my various relations

as one who professes to be a Christian,
as a member of parliament,
as gifted by nature and fortune, as a son, brother, paterfamilias, friend, with influence and powerful connexions.[16]

But Rayrigg proved the wrong place. The Lakes brought a huge number of wealthy tourists each summer, and many turned up at Wilberforce's door when they heard he was in the vicinity. Rather than seclusion he had constant visitors, so many that he decided not to renew the lease on the property when it expired in spring 1789 and, instead, to spend his future summers staying with friends at quieter country retreats. He hungered for a small group of close friends who could support him and pray for him, rather than his current wide group of acquaintances that he no longer felt comfortable with. As such, the letters, prayers and encouragement of John Newton became even more important to him.

Support of Newton

Yes, Sir, you have many praying for you, and among them not a few who are really fervent in prayer, and have the liberty of children at a throne of grace. It is hoped and believed that the Lord has raised you up for the good of His church, and for the good of the nation. This makes you truly a public person, and gives you a place in the hearts of many who never saw you, and whom you will never know.

Communion with God is the great point: whatever is found to have a tendency to damp or indispose our spirits for this, must be either frankly given up, or, if continued, it must be a cross or a burden, which we verily believe it is His pleasure, all things considered, that we for the present should bear.[17]

New Resolve

On 4 October Wilberforce left Rayrigg for Bath, but finding that traditional place of convalescence also busy, on 27 October he finally returned home to London. He had recovered from the brink of death, and learned much about how to maintain himself in the best physical, emotional and spiritual health. At Christmas 1788 he created a new set of rules for his conduct, and found a friend to help him keep to them: 'M. and I made an agreement to pay a guinea forfeit when we broke our rules, and not to tell particulars to each other.'[18]

He also resolved to spend less time in society, and more time focused on God, on maintaining his health, and on the slave trade fight he would now bring to parliament.

New Rules for Conduct

March 1st. Sunday . . . This perpetual hurry of business and company ruins me in soul if not in body. I must make a thorough reform. More solitude and earlier hours – diligence – proper distribution and husbandry of time – associating with religious friends; this will strengthen my weakness by the blessing of God . . . My error hitherto has been, I think, endeavouring to amend this and the other failing, instead of striking at the root of the evil. Let me therefore make a spirited effort, not trusting in myself, but in the strength of the Lord God . . . Rules – As much solitude and sequestration as are compatible with duty. Early hours night and morning. Abstinence as far as health will permit. Regulation of employments for particular times. Prayer three times a day at least, and begin with serious reading or contemplation. Self-denial in little things. Slave trade my main business now.[19]

By spring 1789 he felt ready for the fight. 8 April 1789: 'I resolve to live with a view to health – Slave business – attention to my rules – no waste of eye-sight; and may God bless the work: may my religion be more vital from this retirement.'[20]

The Trade in Flesh and Blood

Key Learning Points

Spiritual Formation

Look after your health. You can only achieve what your body lets you do.

Value solitude. Times alone with God are needed if we are ever to achieve great things for him.

Find an accountability partner. Wilberforce and his friend fined each other when each broke the rules they had set themselves.

Discerning Vision

Listen to advice. Before committing to a project, ask the advice of others who know you well. What do they suggest?

Listen when others recognize a skill in you. They may see it more clearly than you. The early abolitionists saw in Wilberforce their perfect parliamentary leader. What do others say you are good at?

Leadership Skills

Carefully plan your strategy. The committee deliberately chose to work on abolition, not emancipation, as a more achievable goal, and a means towards their ultimate aim.

Do your homework. Wilberforce read, talked with others and learned a huge amount in preparation for the debates.

The Early Debates: 1789–1792

Wilberforce approached the debate with optimism, hopeful MPs would be ashamed by the brutality and suffering associated with the trade, alive to its injustices, and ready to outlaw it. He was disappointed, but resolved to keep on fighting.

Public Propaganda Wars

In April 1789 the Privy Council inquiry set up by Pitt finally published their report into the slave trade, having been interviewing witnesses and examining evidence for twelve months. Clarkson had arranged for a succession of pro-abolition witnesses to give their testimony, but the West India lobby had also been busy in putting forward their counter arguments. The result was a colossal report heavy with invective, but light on recommendations. It set the stage for the coming debate in parliament.

Alongside the enquiry, a battle for public opinion had also begun. As Clarkson toured the country he had set up abolition societies in the major towns and cities he visited, and each began to agitate for the cause. They were helped in this by various high profile supporters. The pottery manufacturer Josiah Wedgwood designed a medallion to be used by the campaign: a kneeling African slave with the words *Am I Not A Man And A Brother?* It became the anti-slavery logo, and was printed on brooches, pamphlets, posters, smoking pipes and anything else the abolitionists could use to get their message out.[1]

The poet William Cowper, a close friend of John Newton, was asked to contribute a poem to the cause. He wrote 'The Negro's Complaint.'

The Abolition Logo

The Negro's Complaint

FORCED from home and all its pleasures,
　　Afric's coast I left forlorn;
To increase a stranger's treasures,
　　O'er the raging billows borne.
Men from England bought and sold me,
　　Paid my price in paltry gold;
But, though slave they have enrolled me,
　　Minds are never to be sold.

Still in thought as free as ever,
　　What are England's rights, I ask,
Me from my delights to sever,
　　Me to torture, me to task?
Fleecy locks and black complexion
　　Cannot forfeit nature's claim;

Skins may differ, but affection
   Dwells in white and black the same.

Why did all-creating nature
   Make the plant, for which we toil?
Sighs must fan it, tears must water,
   Sweat of ours must dress the soil.
Think, ye masters, iron-hearted,
   Lolling at your jovial boards;
Think how many backs have smarted
   For the sweets your cane affords.

Is there, as ye sometimes tell us,
   Is there one who reigns on high?
Has he bid you buy and sell us,
   Speaking from his throne, the sky?
Ask him, if your knotted scourges,
   Matches, blood-extorting screws,
Are the means that duty urges
   Agents of his will to use?

Hark! he answers – wild tornadoes
   Strewing yonder sea with wrecks;
Wasting towns, plantations, meadows,
   Are the voice with which he speaks.
He, foreseeing what vexations
   Afric's sons should undergo,
Fixed their tyrants' habitations
   Where his whirlwinds answer – no.

By our blood in Afric wasted,
   Ere our necks received the chain;
By the miseries that we tasted,
   Crossing in your barks the main;

By our sufferings, since ye brought us
    To the man-degrading mart;
All sustained by patience, taught us
    Only by a broken heart;

Deem our nation brutes no longer,
    Till some reason ye shall find
Worthier of regard and stronger
    Than the colour of our kind.
Slaves of gold, whose sordid dealings
    Tarnish all your boasted powers,
Prove that you have human feelings,
    Ere you proudly question ours!
                    William Cowper, 1788[2]

The most effective contribution came from Plymouth, where an abolition committee created a diagram of a slave ship showing the crowded nature and appalling conditions of a ship on the Middle Passage. The diagram of the *Brookes*, a slave ship registered in Liverpool that regularly took slaves from Africa to Jamaica, became reprinted across the country.[3] (See p. 59.)

First Debate

With all this in the background, on 12 May 1789 Wilberforce finally brought his bill for the abolition of the slave trade to the House of Commons. It was late in the evening when he began his speech, but he spoke for three and a half hours. 'Came to town, sadly unfit for work, but by Divine grace was enabled to make my motion so as to give satisfaction – three hours and a half – I had not prepared

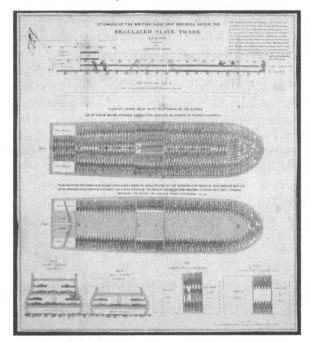

Brookes Diagram

my language, or even gone over all my matter, but being well acquainted with the whole subject I got on.'[4]

He was critical of his speech, but others thought it brilliant. Edmund Burke, himself one of the great parliamentary speakers of the day, described it as 'masterly, impressive and eloquent . . . equal to anything he had ever heard of in modern oratory; and perhaps were not excelled by anything to be met with in Demosthenes'.[5]

Wilberforce gave the House a complete overview of the nature of the trade, of the cruelties of the Middle Passage and the brutal conditions the slaves worked under in the New World, and gave answers to all the perceived objections his opponents would raise. He knew they would claim 1) that the trade acted as a useful training ground for British sailors before they joined the navy, 2) that abolishing it would bring ruin to the national economy, especially to the port cities, and 3) that if the British voted for abolition, the French would only take over the trade, meaning abolition would bring no benefits for Africans, but less money for Britain. He countered with 1) hundreds of sailors actually died on slave ships each year, so banning the trade would prove beneficial to the British navy, 2) people had said losing the American colonies would destroy the British economy, yet Britain continued to prosper after their independence in 1776, and 3) he felt sure that where Britain led the way, France and others would follow.

Excerpts from Wilberforce's Maiden Abolition Speech

I mean not to accuse any one, but to take the shame upon myself, in common, indeed, with the whole parliament of Great Britain, for having suffered this horrid trade to be carried on under their authority. We are all guilty – we ought all to plead guilty, and not to exculpate ourselves by throwing the blame on others . . .

So much misery condensed in so little room, is more than the human imagination has ever before conceived . . .

When the manager shall know that a fresh importation is not to be had from Africa, and that he cannot retrieve the deaths he occasions by any new purchases, humanity must be introduced; an improvement in the system of treating them will thus infallibly be effected, an assiduous care of their health and of their morals, marriage institutions, and many others things as yet little thought of, will take place . . .

The nature and all the circumstances of this trade are now laid open to us; we can no longer plead ignorance, we cannot evade it, it is now an object placed before us, we cannot pass it; we may spurn it, we may kick it out of our way, but we cannot turn aside so as to avoid seeing it; for it is brought now so directly before our eyes that this House must decide, and must justify to all the world, and to their own consciences, the rectitude of the ground and principles of their decision . . . Let not parliament be the only body that is insensible to the principles of national justice. Let us make reparation to Africa, so far as we can, by establishing a trade upon true commercial principles.[6]

Delay Tactics

Since it was late when he finished there was no full debate that night. Nine days later the House came back to the issue, and the abolition opponents made their bid. Despite the Privy Council enquiry of the previous year, they claimed this was an issue of such magnitude the whole House should use actual Commons sessions for a second, more detailed enquiry. Wilberforce was forced to agree, and then watched in horror as the House spent the next four days interviewing just two witnesses. At this rate the whole debate would take years. Parliament then broke for a recess on 23 June, to reconvene in January 1790. His opponents were planning on using delaying tactics to kill off the bill.

That summer a tragedy occurred for the abolition-ists. After Thomas Clarkson, no one had done more for the cause than James Ramsey (the two had often sat up late into the night with Wilberforce, helping him go over evidence and prepare for the debate), and no one had been more criticized. He died in July, worn out from defending himself against the slander his opponents brought against him. The pro-slave trade MP Crisp Molyneux, who in the Commons debates had accused Ramsey's evidence on West Indian slavery conditions of being fabricated, boasted to his son, 'Ramsey is dead – I have killed him.'[7]

The abolitionists had been reliant on Ramsey for up-to-date evidence from the West Indies, but they found a new ally in James Stephen, a lawyer practising in the Caribbean who had hated slavery ever since seeing a female slave burned alive after a sham trial where she was convicted on the flimsiest of evidence. He now took on Ramsey's role of secretly sending information on slave conditions to the abolition committee.

The American and French Revolutions

Two revolutions in the late eighteenth century shook the world and changed the atmosphere around the slavery debate.

United States: In the 1770s the British American colonies rebelled against Britain. The 1776 Declaration of Independence contained the famous phrase, 'we hold these truths to be self-evident, that all men are created equal' and would echo through future decades as slavery was debated. There was always a compro-mise in the creation of the United States between north and south. 'We took each other with our mutual bad habits and respective evils, for better for worse. The northern states adopted us with our slaves, and we adopted them with their Quakers.'[8] Many northern states were committed to outlawing slavery, but it would take a civil war eighty years later for the whole country to follow suit. But the words in the declaration gave hope to slaves everywhere. If white Americans and white British were created equal, then why not white Europeans and black Africans?

France: In the late 1780s the French rebelled against the absolute monarchy of Louis XVI. In 1789 a Parisian mob stormed the Bastille, a royal citadel and prison seen as a symbol of oppression. The populace forced the king to agree to a National Assembly to give ear to their grievances. For a time it seemed France would become the most enlightened and socially progressive regime on earth, and would quickly abolish their slave trade. But in the 1790s, when the revolution became bloody and the Reign of Terror ruled the country, the plight of slaves received a setback. The British began to equate notions of abolition with the anarchy they saw across the Channel, making the cause harder for Wilberforce and his friends.

In summer 1789 Thomas Clarkson was sent by the abolition committee to Paris, hoping to capitalize on the pronouncements coming out of France on liberty, equality and fraternity with a French commitment to abolition. Clarkson was inspired by the movement he saw happening before his eyes: 'In eight or ten days the subject will be brought into the National Assembly. Evidence will not be necessary: and I should not be surprised if the French were to do themselves the honour of voting away this diabolical traffic in a night.'[9] But the vote never came, and events in France eventually cast a huge shadow over abolition efforts in Britain.

West Country Schools

Wilberforce also spent the summer with new friends. Through staying at Clapham he got to know John Thornton's son Henry; his cousin, a fellow MP and a successful banker. Henry in turn introduced him to the famous playwright Hannah More. Both More and Thornton were newly committed evangelicals, and all three found encouragement in each other's company. That summer Wilberforce went to Bath with Thornton, and the two visited Hannah More at her home near Cheddar Gorge. Wilberforce was enraptured by the country scenery, but shocked by the poverty and illiteracy of the locals. One evening at dinner he resolved 'Miss Hannah More, something must be done for Cheddar . . . If you will be at the trouble, I will be at the expense.'[10]

True to his word, over the coming years he gave substantially to the schools that More and her sisters set up to provide free education to the locals. And he persuaded the richer Thornton to give even more. Frequently his letters to More asked how the schools were doing, and how much money they still needed.

Wilberforce's Generosity

As for the expense, the best proof you can give me that you believe me hearty in the cause, or sincere in the wishes expressed in the former part of this letter, is to call on me for money without reserve. Every one should contribute out of his own proper fund. I have more money than time, and if you, or rather your sister, on whom I foresee must be devolved the superintendence of our infant establishment, will condescend to be my almoner, you will enable me to employ some of the superfluity it has pleased God to give me to good purpose.[11]

With schools and the cause of free education, Wilberforce now had three great objects he was working towards: the reformation of manners, the abolition of the slave trade and the education of the West Country. These occupied most of his time, yet he still felt he should be doing much more. He was haunted by the notion he had wasted so much of his life, and therefore wanted to make every moment count.

Impatient for Progress

Jan. 1st 1790 . . . How should I be humbled by seeing the little progress I have made since 1786! Poor Newton dines with me to-day, on whom I then called. He has not dined from home on new-year's day for thirty years. I shall now form a set of rules, and by God's help adhere to them. My health is very bad, a little thing disorders me, at thirty and a half I am in constitution sixty; 'The night cometh when no man can work.'[12]

Slow Progress

By now Wilberforce was the name the public most associated with the cause of abolition. New acquaintances and old friends alike got in touch to offer support. One of them was his old Cambridge University neighbour Thomas Gisborne, now Revd Gisborne. Gisborne also introduced him to another friend, Thomas Babington. Wilberforce began to spend his summer recesses staying with either or both of them, and they also worked with him and Clarkson in going over slave trade evidence, preparing him for the coming debates.

The Final Vote

By early 1791 the parliamentary committee had finished their hearings. The stage was set for another debate, and finally a vote. Wilberforce again spoke powerfully, and was supported by both Prime Minister Pitt and opposition leader Charles Fox. It was rare for Pitt and Fox to agree on anything in the House, but it wasn't enough. Wilberforce had all the best speakers on his side, but not enough MPs. The vote was lost 88 to 163. Parliament had finally spoken.

Commitment to Persevere

Never, never, will we desist till we have wiped away this scandal from the Christian name, released ourselves from the load of guilt, under which we at present labour, and extinguished every trace of this bloody traffic, of which our posterity, looking back to the history of these enlightened times, will scarce believe that it has been suffered to exist so long a disgrace and dishonour to this country.[13]

Sierra Leone Company

That spring, having lost the battle in parliament, Wilberforce and his friends tried a new tactic to support the slaves, and show a different way of trading with Africa. In 1787 Granville Sharp had founded the St George's Bay Company as a means to repatriate ex-slaves to Africa. He couldn't provide employment for all the ex-slaves now living in London (as he had for Jonathan Strong), so he arranged for any who wanted to return to Africa to live in freedom in modern-day Sierra Leone. Four hundred and eleven black Londoners went there in 1787. Sadly, most died from disease but the experiment caught the eye.

In the American War of Independence Britain had promised freedom to any American slaves who came over to the British side and fought against their former masters. After the war the British didn't really know what to do with them. The result was 3,000 Africans living in the freezing conditions of Nova Scotia. They heard of the Sierra Leone haven and asked if they, too, could move there. Henry Thornton became a passionate supporter of the idea and persuaded Wilberforce and Thomas Clarkson to back it. Parliament agreed in May 1791 to the creation of the Sierra Leone Company, with Thornton as chairman.

Clarkson's brother John went to collect the Nova Scotians, and he persuaded over one thousand to come with him to Africa. Thornton believed that free settlers could produce sugar in Sierra Leone at a cheaper price than slaves in the Caribbean. This would undercut the plantation owners, undermine the slave traders and prove to the world that legitimate, profitable trade could take place with Africa. It was an audacious but flawed plan; though Thornton and others spent hundreds of thousands of pounds on the Sierra Leone Company in the coming years, it never yielded a profit. But it did provide a strip on the West African coastline where slave trading was outlawed.

Preparations

Wilberforce spent summer 1791 at Babington's country home, preparing to do battle again in the next year's session. The country was now taking up the cause. The working classes in Britain, due to the agitation of the local abolition societies, the support of many church leaders and the influence of leading artists, began sending petitions to parliament asking for an end to the slave trade. Many people also began boycotting sugar. Wilberforce initially opposed such measures, but came to realize they were necessary for winning over MPs to their cause. He did all he could to exploit these methods for the coming 1792 debate.

Using the Feeling in the Country

I have considered, and talked over with several friends, our future plan of operations, and we are all at length pretty well agreed, that the best course will be to endeavour to excite the flame as much as possible in a secret way, but not to allow it more than to smother until after I shall have given notice of my intention of bringing the subject forward. This must be the signal for the fire's bursting forth. We hope ere that time to have laid all our trains, and that by proper efforts the blaze will then be universal.[14]

The 1792 Debate

In April 1792 Wilberforce again brought to parliament a motion to abolish the slave trade. He made an impassioned and personal speech that night: 'Africa, Africa, your sufferings have been the theme that has arrested and engages my heart – your sufferings no tongue can express; no language impart!'[15] Fox again gave his support, but it was Pitt's oratory that left the Commons spellbound.

Pitt's Speech

Do you think nothing of the ruin and the miseries in which so many other individuals, still remaining in Africa, are involved in consequence of carrying off so many myriads of people? Do you think nothing of their families which are left behind? Of the connections which are broken? Of the friendships, attachments, and relationships that are burst asunder? Do you think nothing of the miseries in consequence, that are felt from generation to generation? . . .

How is this enormous evil ever to be eradicated, if every nation is thus prudentially to wait till the concurrence of all the world shall have been obtained? . . . There is no nation in Europe that has, on the one hand, plunged so deeply into this guilt as Britain; or that is so likely, on the other, to be looked up to as an example, if she should have the manliness to be the first in decidedly renouncing it . . . How much more justly may *other* nations point to *us*, and say, 'Why should we abolish the slave trade, when Great Britain has not abolished?'. . . This is the argument with which we furnish the other nations of Europe, if we again refuse to put an end to the slave trade . . .

Why might not some Roman Senator, reasoning on the principles of some honourable gentlemen, and pointing to *British barbarians*, have predicted with equal boldness, 'There is a people that will never rise to civilization – *there* is a people destined never to be free – a people without the understanding necessary for the attainment of useful arts; depressed by the hand of nature below the level of the human species; and created to form a supply of slaves for the rest of the world.' Might not this have been said . . . as truly of Britain herself . . . as it can now be said by us of the inhabitants of Africa? . . .

We may live to behold the natives of Africa engaged in the calm occupations of industry, in the pursuits of a just and legitimate commerce. We may behold the beams of science and philosophy breaking in upon their land, which, at some happy period in still later times, may blaze with full lustre; and joining their influence to that of pure religion, may illuminate and invigorate the most distant extremities of that immense continent. Then may we hope that even Africa, though last of all the quarters of the globe, shall enjoy at length, in the evening of her days, those blessings which have descended so plentifully upon us in a much earlier period of the world.[16]

As Pitt finished his speech in the early hours, the first light of dawn began streaking through the windows of the Commons chamber. Pitt brilliantly wove this into his speech, and the impact it left on the MPs was stunning.

But, again, it was not enough. Henry Dundas, Secretary of State for Home and Colonial Affairs, and Pitt's close friend, drinking partner and political fixer, proposed an amendment to Wilberforce's bill, that the House should choose to abolish the slave trade 'gradually'. No time limit was put on what 'gradually' would mean, so MPs could assuage their consciences by voting for abolition, but also assuage the business lobby that nothing would change in the foreseeable future. Dundas's amendment was carried; a bill that the slave trade be gradually abolished went through 230 to 85.

Gradual Abolition

I take up my pen for a single moment to inform you that, after a very long debate . . . my motion for immediate Abolition was put by; though supported strenuously by Mr Fox, and by Mr Pitt with more energy and ability than were almost ever exerted in the House of Commons . . . We carried a motion however afterwards for gradual Abolition . . . I am congratulated on all hands, yet I cannot but feel hurt and humiliated. We must endeavour to force the gradual Abolitionists in *their* Bill (for I will never myself bring forward a parliamentary licence to rob and murder) to allow as short a term as possible, and under as many limitations.[17]

Letter to Babington

My present opinion, but I wish for yours, is, that I ought not to allow a longer term than four years, but denounce, if even five were talked of, a determined and vigorous war . . . I rather believe, unless Dundas be forced to it, he will not name any specific time, but hold out the prospect of an accelerated or retarded Abolition

... But my impression is that this must not be allowed, but that the ultimate duration must now be fixed.[18]

Eventually the Commons agreed that 'gradually' meant four years, so the trade would be abolished by 1 January 1796. But having agreed this, nothing was done to implement a timetable towards this date. France grew more anarchic, the Lords delayed their discussions on the bill, the topic became less popular, and the 1796 deadline was ignored when it came around.

Historians have considered these years and debates to have been a golden age in the House of Commons. Wilberforce later reflected, 'Those were glorious nights in the House of Commons.'[19] Speakers of the calibre of Wilberforce, Pitt, Fox and Burke left the house spellbound. Yet all these could not sway enough votes in the chamber. It would be a long, painful and gradual struggle to get the slave trade banned.

The Early Debates

Key Learning Points

Spiritual Formation

 Be generous. 'Every one should contribute out of his own proper fund. I have more money than time.' Which do you have more of? How are you being generous with it?

Find a community of real friends. Wilberforce found the real companionship and support he had been looking for in Henry Thornton and Hannah More.

Discerning Vision

 Always be listening to God. There may be new things he is calling you to. For Wilberforce the Cheddar schools and the Sierra Leone Company were new ventures he was called to take part in.

Leadership Skills

 Vary your tactics. The legislation angle failed, so the abolitionists set up the Sierra Leone Company. It was a different means to work towards the same end.

The right leader is key. The West Country schools could not have been created without Hannah More's leadership. The more important the role, the more important it is you find the right person.

Mission Skills

Use creativity in campaigns. Use the media and art worlds to help spread your message, with logos, poems, songs, speeches, posters and more.

Petition and boycott. These are two simple ways to call people to action. Link the everyday commodity (e.g. sugar) with a global injustice (e.g. slave trade) for the greatest effect in boycotts.

Don't blame others. Focus on solutions rather than scapegoats. Wilberforce chose not to get drawn into an argument by blaming the slave traders. He emphasized the responsibility of us all in an immoral system, and argued for change.

Clapham Joy, Westminster Despair: 1792–1797

The coming years were filled with more political defeats for Wilberforce. But these were balanced by a domestic move to Clapham to live with his friends in a unique form of community, and then eventually to a very happy marriage.

Move to Clapham

John Thornton died in 1790. In May 1792 his son Henry built a home at Clapham named Battersea Rise. The property was so large he built two other homes on the grounds: Broomfield, which he let out to Pitt and Wilberforce's mutual friend Edward Eliot; and Glenelg, let out to Charles Grant, chairman of the East India Company. Wilberforce moved in with Thornton at the main house; they now lived together at Battersea Rise as their country house and at Old Palace Yard opposite parliament as their town house.

The network of friendships centred around Wilberforce and Thornton now had a fixed geographical base at Clapham, and later generations named their community the Clapham Sect. Not all the members lived at Clapham, but all visited frequently. The network became a unique Christian community, sharing their homes and holidays, treating each other as members of one large extended family, and working together on a series of measures motivated by their faith, of which abolition of the slave trade was the foremost.

Members of the Clapham Sect

William Wilberforce: Politician; parliamentary leader of the abolition cause; campaigner on a number of other issues.

Henry Thornton: Successful and wealthy banker; an MP and adviser to the government on economic theory; chairman of the Sierra Leone Company; treasurer of a number of Clapham Sect initiatives.

Hannah More: Successful writer who had plays performed at the West End in London but became disillusioned with London society life and moved to the West Country; she and her sisters ran a series of schools providing free education; she wrote numerous stories and pieces of literature on behalf of the Clapham Sect.

James Stephen: Lawyer practising in Barbados until 1797, then moved to Clapham; provided the Clapham Sect with detailed information on the barbaric conditions of slavery in the West Indies; helped Wilberforce draft many of his bills.

Zachary Macaulay: Governor of Sierra Leone who moved to Clapham in 1799; secretary for a number of Clapham Sect initiatives; editor of the *Christian Observer* and the *Anti-Slavery Reporter*.

Charles Grant: Chairman of the East India Company; provided information to the Clapham Sect on conditions in India.

Lord Teignmouth: Governor-General of British India; provided information on conditions in India; became President of the Bible Society.

John Venn: Vicar of Clapham; preached many of the sermons they listened to each Sunday and provided spiritual leadership and encouragement to the group.

Thomas Gisborne: Clergyman, poet, philosopher and writer based at Yoxhall Lodge in Staffordshire.

Thomas Babington: Country gentleman who owned Rothley Temple in Leicestershire, later an MP; led a parliamentary campaign to ban the lottery.

There were others they worked with, such as Thomas and John Clarkson, Granville Sharp, and later on Thomas Fowell Buxton, but the above group were a core community who lived in each other's houses, shared their lives with each other, and worked as brothers and sisters on a series of measures that changed the world.

Henry Thornton's Clapham Experiment

On the whole, I am in hopes some good may come out of our Clapham system. Wilberforce is a candle that should not be hid under a bushel. The influence of his conversation is, I think, great and striking. I am surprised to find how much religion everybody seems to have when they get into our house. They all seem to submit, and to acknowledge the advantage of a religious life, and we are not at all queer or guilty of carrying things too far.

Description of Clapham Life

Presently, streaming from adjoining villas or crossing the common, appeared others who, like Henry Thornton, had spent an occupied day in town, and now resorted to this well-known garden to gather up their families and enjoy a pleasant hour. Hannah More is there, with her sparkling talk . . . and the long-faced, blue-eyed Scotsman [Grant], with his fixed, calm look, unchanged as an aloe tree, known as the Indian Director, one of the kings of Leadenhall Street; and the gentle Thane, Lord Teignmouth, whose easy talk flowed on, like a southern brook, with a sort of drowsy murmur; and Macaulay stands by listening, silent, with hanging eyebrows; and Babington, in blue coat, dropping weighty words with husky voice; and young listeners . . . the young Grants, and young Stephen . . .

But whilst these things are talked of in the shade, and the knot of wise men draw close together, in darts the member for Yorkshire [Wilberforce] from the green fields to the south, like a sunbeam into a shady room, and the faces of the old brighten, and the children clap their hands with joy. He joins the group of elders, catches up a thread of their talk, dashes off a bright remark, pours a ray of happy illumination, and for a few moments seems as wise, as thoughtful, and as constant as themselves. But this dream will not last and these watchful young eyes know it. They remember that he is as restless as they are, as fond of fun and movement. So, on the first youthful challenge, away flies the volatile statesman. A bunch of flowers, a ball, is thrown in sport, and away dash, in joyous rivalry, the children and the philanthropist. Law and statesmanship forgotten, he is the gayest child of them all.

But presently, when the group has broken up, and the friends have gone to their houses, the circle under Henry Thornton's roof gathers for its evening talk. In the Oval Library, which Pitt planned, niched and fringed all round with books, looking out on the pleasant lawn, they meet for more sustained conversation. In this easy intercourse even the shy Gisborne opens himself. At times the talk is interspersed with reading, the books chosen by the host . . .[20]

Missionaries to India

One of the causes the Clapham Sect took up alongside the abolition of the slave trade was to improve conditions in British India. The East India Company held a monopoly on all trade with India, and acted as final authority for all matters there. They showed a great reluctance to do anything to improve the conditions of the millions

of Indians they were exploiting, for fear it would inter-
fere with their profits. But through their relationship with
Charles Grant, the Clapham Sect became determined to
bring education and Christianity to India.

In 1793 the Company charter was due for renewal.
Wilberforce lobbied the government for the minor step of
sending chaplains for the English officials of the Company
(currently there were none). When this was granted he
went further, and got clauses for the East India Company
directors to be able to send out missionaries and set up
schools for the Indian population. Dundas agreed to all
this, and promised to guide the bill through parliament.
But then a reverse occurred. The Company realized that
providing education could result in the Indians seeking
further improvements in their working conditions, so they
lobbied Dundas to change the conditions. Rather than
sending missionaries to India, they actually made it illegal
for any missionaries to go out there, whether to preach or
to set up schools.

Indian Defeat

The East India directors and proprietors have
triumphed – all my clauses were last night struck out on
the third reading of the Bill, (with Dundas's consent!!
this is *honour*,) and our territories in Hindostan, twenty
millions of people included, are left in the undisturbed
and peaceable possession, and committed to the provi-
dential protection of – Brama.[21]

The charter was renewed for another twenty years; it
would be 1813 at the earliest before Wilberforce could
again do anything to improve the living conditions of

millions of Indians, many of whom lived in virtual slavery to the Company.

Slave Trade Defeats

The abolition cause also continued to experience defeats. The 1792 bill for gradual abolition had passed through the Commons, but the House of Lords still had to approve it, and they insisted on their own right to also call witnesses before voting. In 1793 they called seven, and in 1794 just two. The bill was being quietly dropped.

Wilberforce started to experience personal danger due to his involvement. Captain Kimber had been singled out in the 1792 debate as a captain who expressed undue cruelty to his slaves. He was tried for the murder of a slave girl on one of his ships, but was acquitted, according to Wilberforce 'through the shameful remissness of the Crown lawyers, and the indecent behaviour of a high personage who from the bench identified himself with the prisoner's cause'.[22] When Kimber's trial was over he confronted Wilberforce demanding money and threatening violence. Wilberforce had armed guards protect him for a time, but he reasoned Kimber was unlikely to carry out his threats: 'I really believe, that if he were to commit any act of violence it would be beneficial rather than injurious to the cause.'[23]

Conditions also worsened for the abolitionists as conditions in France worsened. In summer 1792 the French put Louis XVI on trial. He was executed on 21 January 1793, and just eleven days later the French declared war on Britain plus most of Europe. The French Revolution was tearing the country apart, and the British aristocracy equated the principles of liberty for slaves with the anarchy and terror they saw across the English Channel.

Unpopularity of Abolition

I do not imagine that we could meet with twenty persons in Hull at present who would sign a petition, that are not republicans. People connect democratical principles with the Abolition of the Slave Trade, and will not hear it mentioned. This is I hear precisely the case in Norfolk.[24]

But Wilberforce refused to abandon the campaign simply because it was unpopular. With the 1792 bill stuck in the Lords, he resolutely brought a new bill each year to the Commons. In 1793 and 1794 he tried a bill to eliminate the foreign slave trade; in 1795 he reverted to full abolition and lost 78 to 61. By now, apart from the Clapham Sect, he had few supporters; Thomas Clarkson suffered a nervous breakdown and moved to the Lake District to recover; the abolition committee stopped meeting. From the early fighters, it seemed only Wilberforce was now still committed to the campaign.

Political Matters

Wilberforce had never limited himself to involvement on just one issue, and he continued to attend far more parliamentary debates than most of his colleagues, always voting in accordance with his conscience. This practice soon made him even more isolated.

In early 1795 he argued for making peace with France, and publicly opposed Pitt for the first time. He was criticized and misunderstood by many of his friends, and publicly ignored by the King at a state occasion. The opposition of Fox boasted he had gone over to them.

In truth he was simply voting in the independent way he always approached each issue. The opposition were shocked when he went back to the government side to vote for Pitt's Seditious Assemblies Bill, a measure banning public meetings of more than fifty people, and requiring a magistrate's licence for discussing political matters at public events. Wilberforce was roundly criticized for campaigning for freedoms abroad whilst voting for repressive legislation at home, to which he answered, 'I do not willingly support these Bills, but I look on them as a temporary sacrifice, by which the blessings of liberty may be transmitted to our children unimpaired.'[25]

Through this support his friendship with Pitt was restored, and he borrowed Pitt's carriage to make a last-minute journey to York in November 1795 to address a hostile meeting that opposed Pitt's bill. He raced from London to York in two days, when it usually took four. He surprised Pitt's opponents with his appearance, made a devastating speech supporting the Prime Minister, and swung the Yorkshire public opinion back behind Pitt.

Despite all this high political drama, his first concern was still how to best serve God. That November he started the practice of making 'launchers', questions or comments he could use at dinner parties or with individuals to turn the conversation to spiritual matters. He campaigned for the well-being of people across the globe, but he also sought to be an evangelist at home.

Closer Than Ever

By 1796 he felt a small measure of optimism. He had shown that he was no revolutionary by supporting Pitt's gagging measures, and the time of Dundas's deadline had been reached. Wilberforce brought an abolition bill in February 1796.

The Timing of 1796

Mr Jenkinson: 'I anxiously wish that the question were postponed at least till the return of peace.'

Wilberforce: 'There is something not a little provoking in the dry, calm way in which gentlemen are apt to speak of the sufferings of others. The question suspended! Is the desolation of wretched Africa suspended? Are all the complicated miseries of this atrocious trade – is the work of death suspended? No, sir, I will not delay this motion, and I call upon the House not to insult the forbearance of Heaven by delaying this tardy act of justice.'[26]

The bill got through the first reading. His opponents moved forward the timing of its second reading to get it thrown out during a quiet sitting. Wilberforce was told of this one evening at Old Palace Yard: 'Hurried from dinner at home over to House, to the second reading of the Slave Bill. Spoke against time till many came. Carried it 63 to 31.'[27] He could play the parliamentary games as well as they could by now.

A third reading would see the bill clear the Commons. 'Dined before House. Slave Bill thrown out by 74 to 70, ten or twelve of those who had supported me absent in the country, or on pleasure. Enough at the Opera to have carried it. Very much vexed and incensed at our opponents.'[28] Six supportive MPs had gone to the opening night of a new comic opera in nearby Covent Garden. With their support the bill would have passed, but they had decided a night out was more important than the freedom of 40,000 innocent annual victims. That night in his diary he confided, 'I am permanently hurt about the Slave Trade.'[29]

He became ill and despondent, but then had to throw himself into a general election campaign in May 1796, with all the constant travel and speeches in Yorkshire that entailed. He retained his seat, but was exhausted by the time of the summer recess.

Becoming an Author

The defeats of this period made Wilberforce more determined to do something further on his other great purpose in life – the reformation of society through the spreading of Christianity. Since 1793 he had been working in spare moments on a book that would articulate his religious beliefs to the world. The title was hardly calculated to set pulses racing: *A Practical View of the Prevailing Religious System of Professed Christians, in the Higher and Middle Classes in This Country, Contrasted with Real Christianity.* His publisher told him that religious books never sold well, and assumed it would be published under a pseudonym. 'You mean to put your name to the work? Then I think we may venture upon 500 copies.'[30]

The book contrasted the living Christianity of Wilberforce and his evangelical friends, centred on 'Looking unto Jesus!'[31] with the nominalism preached in so many churches, and loosely followed by most of the aristocracy. It proved a best seller: 7,500 copies were sold in the first six months after publication in April 1797, and by 1826 it had gone through 15 editions in Britain, and 25 in the United States.

A Practical View of Christianity

The grand radical defect in the practical system of these nominal Christians, is their forgetfulness of all the peculiar doctrines of the Religion which they profess – the corruption of human nature – the atonement of the Saviour – and the sanctifying influence of the Holy Spirit.[22]

He was congratulated by all his friends on a great success, a book that all the establishment began talking about.

Reactions to His Book

Lord Muncaster: I heartily thank you for your book. As a friend I thank you for it; as a man I doubly thank you; but as a member of the Christian world, I render you all gratitude and acknowledgment. I thought I knew you well, but I know you better now, my dearest excellent Wilber.[33]

John Newton: I deem it the most valuable and important publication of the present age that I have seen: especially as it is yours. There are many persons both in church and state, who, from their situations, are quite inaccessible to us little folks: what we preach they do not hear, what we write they will not read. But your book must and will be read.[34]

John Newton: What a phenomenon has Mr Wilberforce sent abroad! Such a book by such a man, and at such a time![35]

Wilberforce's Response to Newton

I cannot help saying it is a great relief to my mind to have published what I may call my manifesto; to have plainly told my worldly acquaintance what I think of their system and conduct, and where it must end . . . I shall at least feel a solid satisfaction from having openly declared myself as it were on the side of Christ, and having avowed on what my hopes for the well-being of the country bottom.[36]

Henry Thornton wrote to Hannah More that 'Burke spent much of the two last days of his life in reading Wilberforce's book, and said that he derived much comfort from it, and that if he lived he should thank Wilberforce for having sent such a book into the world.'[37] Everyone seemed to be discussing it. Wilberforce dealt with his success by praying for humility for himself, and blessing upon others.

Journal Entry: Easter Sunday, 16 April 1797

Look back on the mercies of God through life. Oh how numerous, and how freely bestowed! Try Quintilian's plan (Phantasia) as to Christ's crucifixion. Pray for pardon, acceptance, holiness, peace; for courage, humility, and all that I chiefly want; for love and heavenly-mindedness. Pray to be guided aright respecting my domestic choice, &c. Pray for my country both in temporal and spiritual things. Pray for political wisdom; for the success of my book just come out; for the poor slaves; for the Abolition; for Sierra Leone; for the success of missions. Think over my enemies with forgiveness and love, over my friends and acquaintances, and pray for both. In the evening make launchers, and think how I may do good to my acquaintances and friends, and pray for wisdom here.[38]

A Whirlwind Courtship

By Easter 1797 Wilberforce was in Bath, and felt a strong need to pray for a greater focus on Jesus. His mind was constantly being filled with a young woman. Thomas Babington introduced him to a young lady called Barbara Spooner, and he couldn't stop thinking about her. Within eight days of meeting he had proposed. Within three months they were married, and it would have been earlier had Pitt not summoned him back to London to help deal with a naval mutiny that threatened Britain's security. This man who was so cautious in committing to different political campaigns had fallen head over heels in love.

Barbara was twenty when they married, and he thirty-eight. But the age difference didn't seem to matter. They became a very happy couple.

Barbara Spooner

I believe indeed she is admirably suited to me, and there are many circumstances which seem to advise the step. I trust God will bless me; I go to pray to Him. I believe her to be a real Christian, affectionate, sensible, rational in habits, moderate in desires and pursuits; capable of bearing prosperity without intoxication, and adversity without repining.[39]

They took a honeymoon at Cheddar Gorge, so he could show his wife the schools he cared so passionately about and gave so generously towards, and so they could start their marriage with a sense of gratitude for all the blessings they had compared to others less fortunate.

Honeymoon at Cheddar

Received at Cowslip Green with great kindness – delightful day and sweet ride. Sunday morning, as early as able, tour of the schools – Shipham, Axbridge, and Cheddar. Delighted with all we saw, Cheddar in particular.[40]

Henry Thornton had married the previous year, so all was now joy and domestic bliss at Clapham. Sadness came with the unexpected death of Edward Eliot in September 1797, but Thornton let Broomfield to the newly married Wilberforces. The families still lived on the same property, if not quite in the same house.

Clapham Joy, Westminster Despair

Key Learning Points

Spiritual Formation

Share life with others. The Clapham Sect formed a unique community – they lived together, holidayed together and even raised their children together. They were friends who truly shared life together.

Don't be ashamed of Christ. Wilberforce declared himself openly on the side of Christ with his book. His reputation grew rather than shrank.

Marry for love. Whirlwind romances don't always lead to happy marriages . . . but sometimes they do!

Discerning Vision

Don't ignore injustices. Wilberforce campaigned for slaves abroad, but voted for the Seditious Assemblies Bill that curtailed freedom of speech for the working classes at home. He could have done more to speak out for the freedoms of his countrymen.

Leadership Skills

Form a team of different skills. The Clapham Sect achieved so much because they were a combination of politicians, businesspeople, lawyers, editors, writers and church leaders all working together.

Be wary of opponents. Dundas let Wilberforce down. Not all promises can be trusted.

Persevere. Don't give up on something just because it's unpopular. It may be all the more necessary.

Mission Skills

Make 'launchers'. How can you bring Christ relevantly into conversations?

Be creative in communicating Christ. *Practical View* reached people that launchers could not reach.

Outside Interests: 1797–1804

Wilberforce continued to campaign on the slave trade, but with his friends at Clapham also became involved in the beginning of several other ventures that aimed to further the work of God, including the Church Missionary Society, the Bible Society, and the *Christian Observer* magazine.

Church Missionary Society

The group had discussed the formation of a missionary society on many previous occasions. Wilberforce had obtained permissions for missionaries to be sent to Australia, and they had lobbied hard for sending them to India. But permission was only half the battle; even when parliament opened the door, sometimes there were no missionaries to be sent. Creating a society to recruit missionaries was therefore regularly on the Clapham agenda. 'Dined and slept at Battersea Rise for Missionary meeting – Simeon – Charles Grant – Venn. Something, but not much, done – Simeon in earnest.'[1]

The discussions continued, and in 1799 the group formed the Society for Missions to Africa and the East, which later became the Church Missionary Society. Wilberforce, Thornton and Babington were all key members, and used the society to recruit for their missionary dreams for Sierra Leone, India, Australia and beyond.

Continued Work on Slave Trade

The war with France threw up new issues within the slave trade, and new disagreements with Pitt. Britain had recently occupied several French West Indian islands. The French revolutionaries had outlawed slavery on the islands, but the British government now allowed slaves to be reintroduced to newly acquired Trinidad and St Vincent.

Wilberforce seemed unsure how to confront Pitt over this betrayal of the abolitionist cause, until James Stephen wrote and goaded him into action: 'Lloyd's Coffee House is in a roar of merriment, at the dextrous compromise Mr Pitt has made between his religious friends and his and Dundas's West India supporters.'[2]

Wilberforce finally spoke with Pitt and got the orders revoked. But Stephen was still not satisfied it had taken Wilberforce so long to be prompted into action.

Stephen's Criticism

I still clearly think that you have been improperly silent, and that when you see the government loading the bloody altars of commerce, the idol of this Carthage, with an increase of human victims, and building new altars for the same execrable purpose, while the sword of Almighty vengeance seems uplifted over us for that very offence, you are bound by the situation wherein you have placed yourself to

cry aloud against it. You are even the rather bound
to do so, because those high priests of Moloch, Lord
Liverpool and Mr Dundas, are your political, and Mr
Pitt also your private friend.[3]

Stephen had recently returned from the West Indies,
committed to doing all he could to help the struggling
abolition efforts. He felt he was risking his friendship
with Wilberforce by writing to him so critically, but his
honesty actually brought them closer. 'Go on, my dear
sir, and welcome. Believe me, I wish you not to abate any
thing of the force or frankness of your animadversions .
. . Openness is the only foundation and preservative of
friendship.'[4]

The two became great friends through the coming years,
and became family in 1800 when Stephen married Wilberforce's sister Sarah.

Strained Relationship with Pitt

In May 1798 Wilberforce's relationship with Pitt became
even more strained. An MP called George Tierney opposed
Pitt in the Commons, and Pitt accused him of 'obstructing
the defence of the country'.[5] Tierney demanded satisfaction in the way many gentlemen did in those days, and
the two fought a duel on Putney Heath. Both fired two
shots and missed, and considered the matter settled. But
Wilberforce was horrified, firstly that the Prime Minister should endanger his life in a duel, and secondly that
the whole affair took place on a Sunday. He immediately
tabled a motion in the Commons that duelling be made
illegal.

Letter from Pitt

I feel it a real duty to say to you frankly that your motion is one for my removal. If any step on the subject is proposed in parliament and agreed to, I shall feel from that moment that I can be of more use out of office than in it; for in it, according to the feelings I entertain, I could be of none. I state to you, as I think I ought, distinctly and explicitly what I feel.

Wilberforce backed down and withdrew his motion. He had no desire to see Pitt out of office, and having made his point he could feel that he, too, had received 'satisfaction' over the incident.

He continued to oppose Pitt on other matters though. He argued for exemptions for the poorest from Pitt's Income Tax Bill, and successfully obtained an exemption for Methodists living on Jersey from having to do military drills on a Sunday. Wilberforce had become a passionate believer in the importance of taking a proper Sabbath day off each week, and fought for others to have the privilege. He constantly lamented his own lack of time for solitude.

Journal Entries

Jan. 14th 1798. [Over Christmas] time was frittered away in calls and dining out. Let me try to get more time for meditation and Scripture. I have read barely a chapter each day through this hurrying week. Dining out every day has a bad effect on the mind; I will try to dine at home, at least once, and if I can twice every week . . . Entire solitude I find a different thing from even being with my wife only; it seems to give me over more entirely to the power, and throw me more absolutely upon the mercy, of God.[7]

April 15th 1798. I resolve to be up in time to have an hour before breakfast for serious meditation, prayer, and Scripture preparation for these dangerous times; also more time for unbroken thought; half or three-quarters of an hour on parliamentary topics.[8]

Wilberforce never had time to himself due to the huge number of causes he took on, his sense of diligence in attending almost all the parliamentary debates taking place, his commitment to faithfully representing his Yorkshire constituents, and his homes at Old Palace Yard and Battersea Rise always being open to any visitors, MPs and activists who came to pay him a visit or ask for a favour. Thornton and other friends constantly chastised him for seeing too many people, but Wilberforce's generosity meant he couldn't turn away any visitor, and found it difficult to turn down any worthwhile cause.

Thornton's Complaint

Wilberforce has bought a house near Bath, which I a little lament, on the ground of the bad economy of it; for he is a man, who, were he in Norway or Siberia, would find himself infested by company; since he would even produce a population, for the sake of his society, in the regions of the earth where it is the least.

His heart also is so large that he never will be able to refrain from inviting people to his house. The quiet and solitude he looks to will, I conceive, be impossible, and the Bath house will be troubled with exactly the same heap of fellows as the Battersea Rise one.[9]

But abolition was always his priority. In 1798 he thought he had achieved a breakthrough, but was again disappointed: 'Busy preparing for Slave motion, which made. Fox, Grey, Sheridan, &c came. Thought we had carried it – 83 to 87.'[10] In 1799 he lost by 54 to 84. The West India lobby had by now at least conceded that the trade was filled with violence and immorality, but they maintained it was necessary for the British economy, and they continued to have the support of large numbers of MPs.

The year 1800 was the first since 1790 that he didn't bring a bill; the government was negotiating with France over a possible end to the war, and abolition was one of the terms in the proposed treaty. Wilberforce didn't bring a bill to the Commons so as not to interrupt the discussions. But they came to nothing, the war continued, and so did the slave trade.

Pitt's Resignation

On 16 February 1801 a political earthquake happened. William Pitt, Prime Minister for seventeen years, resigned his office. Ireland had just voted to join Great Britain in political union, creating the nation of the United Kingdom. Pitt had promised Irish Catholics they would receive equal voting rights with Protestants, but King George III vetoed this. Pitt felt he had to resign on a matter of principle.

It threw the political scene into turmoil. Henry Addington became Prime Minister, and politicians of all sides wondered if they would be included in his new Cabinet. Even Wilberforce succumbed to thinking of what could be, and required a Sunday at home to remember he was called to higher things than a place in government.

Blessings of Keeping Sabbath

I was for a little intoxicated, and had risings of ambition. Blessed be God for this day of rest and religious occupation, wherein earthly things assume their true size and comparative insignificance; ambition is stunted, and I hope my affections in some degree rise to things above.[11]

He wasn't called to hold office, but to fight for the rights of the disenfranchised from an independent position. And there were plenty of causes he still needed to fight on. The high taxes required for the war effort, combined with a series of bad harvests, meant many of the poorest in the country were literally starving. Wilberforce always gave generously to those in need, and now he became all the more concerned for the poorest in Yorkshire.

Letter to his Constituency Agent

I have heard however that Pudsey and its neighbourhood are in extreme distress, and that scarcely any merchants or gentlemen live in that parish. I have therefore resolved to beg you to apply any sum not exceeding £50 for their relief. I cannot get any bill to-day, but I will send you one shortly.[12]

In 1801, due to the poor harvests and the poverty, he refrained again from bringing an abolition bill, so as not to appear insensitive to the charge of being concerned for slaves abroad but not for the destitute at home.

The *Christian Observer*

Hannah More's commitment to the West Country schools led the Clapham Sect to think what more they could do to educate the country. More had also written short stories for the working populace – cheap tracts to give those who had previously been illiterate something to read, and something to counter the radical ideals of the French Revolution that were circulating. Now the Sect went further, creating a monthly magazine that would help spread their ideas and aid their campaigns on abolition, missions, education and whatever else they planned.

Zachary Macaulay became editor and contributed most of the articles, but his dry style needed something else to enliven it. Wilberforce contributed some articles, and took responsibility for getting other writers on board.

Letter to Hannah More

You may perhaps at first suspect some laying of heads together, when you read what I am about to propose to you – that you should lend your aid a little to the cause of the *Christian Observer* . . . *my* idea was, and is, that you should write some religious and moral novels, stories, tales, call 'em what you will, illustrative of character and principles. The Cheap Repository tales, a little raised in their subjects, are the very things

I want; and I am persuaded, if you would thus give your aid, and I join mine, (which I will if you will agree to furnish your complement,) we might at once greatly raise the character and increase the utility of the work. The truth is, it is heavy, and it will be heavy from the very nature of the case. If it be not enlivened it will sink, and you will hereafter regret that you refused to lend a helping hand to keep it above water. Do therefore think of what I say, and fall to work. Notwithstanding your ill health, you have no valid excuse for not taking up the pen, because you write with such facility. I who, without any false humility, must say the very opposite of myself, will yet fall to work when I know you have agreed to contribute. You must not refuse me.[13]

Further Fruitless Years

The Addington administration showed no signs of doing anything on the slave trade, but in 1802 George Canning, a rising star from Pitt's previous government, promised to bring a bill to prevent slaves being brought in to the new West Indian possessions Britain had taken from the French. This would prevent the sort of cases that Pitt had so nearly allowed four years previously in St Vincent and Trinidad. Wilberforce decided to support Canning's bill, and then build on that momentum with his own usual bill for full abolition.

But the motion failed. 'Canning's motion – House flat – the motion sadly too short . . . I grieved to the heart.'[14] And it was now too late in the session for Wilberforce to bring his own bill. Another year had passed without the Commons even having the opportunity to vote for full abolition. The same happened in 1803: Napoleon, the new

French Emperor, was threatening invasion, and parliament was more concerned with defending the coastline than considering the welfare of slaves. 'You can conceive what would be said by Lord Hawkesbury & Co. if I were to propose the Abolition now, when the whole attention of government is justly called to the state of the country.'[15] It was now four years since he had brought a bill. The cause seemed more hopeless than ever.

Bible Society

But in 1803 there was another cause that Wilberforce and the Clapham Sect took on. They were already supporters of The Religious Tract Society, that distributed Christian and wholesome literature to the working classes. Many of Hannah More's cheap novels were among those given out by the Society, and Zachary Macaulay was the RTS Clapham correspondent.

At an RTS meeting in London the Society heard of the scarcity of Bibles in rural Wales, in particular the story of Mary Jones, a 15-year-old girl who saved money for six years, and then walked twenty-eight miles over the Welsh mountains to be able to finally buy her own copy of the Scriptures. A Welsh Sunday school teacher, Thomas Charles, suggested a separate society be formed to distribute bibles, and the idea of the Bible Society was born.

The Birth of the Bible Society

Thomas Charles: I beg you to consider establishing a Society similar to the RTS to supply cheap Bibles to Wales.

> Joseph Hughes: Surely a Society might be formed for such a purpose, and if for Wales, why not also for the Empire and for the world?

The group agreed and, realizing they needed help in funds, expertise and connections, approached Wilberforce and Charles Grant: '[5 April 1803] Hughes, Reyner, and Grant breakfasted with me [Wilberforce] on Bible Society formation.' Wilberforce was impressed with the idea, and the group met again a few days later to sketch out a plan.

Founding the Bible Society

A few of us met together at Mr Hardcastle's counting-house, at a later hour than suited city habits, out of regard to my convenience, and yet on so dark a morning that we discussed by candle-light, while we resolved upon the establishment of the Bible Society.

Wilberforce insisted on proper research to find out whether there was a real demand for giving out bibles. Questions were sent across the country and across to mainland Europe.

Wilberforce's Bible Questionnaire

1. Can the poor in your neighbourhood read?
2. To what extent are they furnished with the Holy Scriptures?
3. Do they discover a solicitude to read them?
4. What has been done towards supplying this want?
5. Are there persons in your neighbourhood willing further to encourage the distribution of the Holy Scriptures in our own and in foreign lands?

The answers were overwhelming, so the British & Foreign Bible Society was formed. Wilberforce turned down the offered role of Chair since he was already so involved in other pursuits, but he regularly advocated for the Society, and gave generously. The Clapham Sect swung into full support, with Henry Thornton becoming Treasurer, and the ever faithful Zachary Macaulay doing much of the work. Granville Sharp chaired the public meetings. Lord Teignmouth was President, and said the role was the most important post he had ever held – more important than Governor-General of India.

Outside Interests

Key Learning Points

Spiritual Formation

Be honest in friendships. Real friends are able to give and receive criticism and still remain close.

Keep a Sabbath. Take one full day off each week, to rest and spend time with your family.

Be compassionate. Wilberforce was generous with his time to visitors and those in need who came to his door, and generous with his money when the poor were in need.

Discerning Vision

Discern personal ambition from God's call. Wilberforce was tempted to think of a Cabinet role for himself, but realized God was calling him to other things.

Don't be afraid of a big vision. 'If for Wales, why not for the Empire and the whole world!'

Research new projects. Before committing to the Bible Society idea, Wilberforce and friends undertook research to establish whether there was a real need for such a thing.

Leadership Skills

Manage your time. Know what to say no to, so you can say a wholehearted yes to other things.

Mission Skills

 Keep in touch. In any movement, people need regular updates on what's happening to stay committed. The *Christian Observer* enabled the Clapham Sect to regularly update supporters around the country of their different campaigns.

West Indian Abolition: 1804–1807

In 1804 Wilberforce brought his first abolition bill to the Commons in four years. It proved an unexpected success, and within three years both Commons and Lords had finally voted to outlaw the slave trade. After twenty years campaigning, the abolitionists won.

Renewing the Fight

Since Wilberforce's previous abolition bill of 1799, the House of Commons had been swelled by 100 Irish MPs. Most had no direct interest in the slave trade, and they certainly didn't have constituents whose jobs depended on it. On 30 May 1804, when Wilberforce brought his bill, he had 100 new hearers who were open to persuasion. He also had a supportive Prime Minister; twenty days earlier the King had removed Addington and again called on Pitt to lead the government.

The 1804 Debate

I never felt so discomposed, and stiff, and little at ease on any former occasion, and I own I think I did not do near so well as usual, though the Speaker said he hoped I had satisfied myself, as I had done every body else. The anti-abolitionists made no stand in speaking . . . We divided 124 against 49. All the Irish members voted with us. There was a great Irish dinner, 33 or 34 dining together.[1]

The abolitionists won the second reading, too, 100 to 42 on 7 June 1804. They now worked feverishly at Wilberforce's house, planning for the final debate and tallying lists of supportive MPs. They had a new recruit to the inner circle in Henry Brougham, a young Scottish lawyer: 'Brougham, Stephen, Babington, Henry Thornton, Macaulay, dining with us in Palace Yard most days of the Slave Trade debates.'[2] They feared the rumours many of their new Irish supporters would vote against them on the third reading. 'June 23rd. The Irish members, who at first all so warm for Abolition, have since been persuaded by some West Indians that it is an invasion of private property.'[3]

But on 27 June they prevailed, and carried the vote 99 to 33. The Commons had finally passed a bill to end the slave trade with immediate effect. Now they just needed to repeat the process in the Lords.

Progress at Last

I fear the House of Lords! But it seems as if He, who has the hearts of all men in his power, was beginning to look with pity on the sufferings of those poor oppressed fellow-creatures whose cause I assert. I shall ever reckon it the greatest of all my temporal favours, that I have been providentially led to take the conduct of this business.[4]

As an MP Wilberforce couldn't lead the battle in the Lords himself. He now needed someone else who might also be 'providentially led to take the conduct of this business'. He quickly resolved on William Grenville, who had been present back in 1787 when Pitt encouraged him to take up the cause, and who was now Lord Grenville.

Letter to William Grenville

My dear Lord Grenville,
Though I have been so long in parliament, I was ignorant till yesterday evening, when I accidentally learned it in conversing with the Bishop of London, that in the House of Lords a bill from the House of Commons is in a destitute and orphan state, unless it has some peer to adopt and take the conduct of it. So soon as I knew this, your Lordship occurred to me as the natural guardian and protector of the Bill for the Abolition of the Slave Trade. I know not whether you may happen to recollect, that it was by advice of you and Pitt that I went down to the House of Commons, and gave notice of my intention of bringing forward a proposition on that subject, which in private had long engaged my attention; and you took a leading part in drawing up the resolutions, on which we grounded our measure. Let me earnestly entreat you therefore to undertake this pious charge.[5]

Grenville agreed to the task, but both he and Pitt advised they should delay until 1805. The parliamentary session was now nearing the summer recess, and both felt that without proper time to examine the issue, and again call witnesses if they chose, the Lords were more likely to simply vote against the bill.

Delaying the Lords' Bill

Pitt told me that a meeting had been held of the Cabinet, in which it was agreed that the subject to be hung up till next year, on the ground that the examination of evidence indispensable; that they could make no progress this year, and that therefore it was better not to bring it on. That it was best for the cause to be regarded as a new question, on the ground of the danger of the colonies; and this more likely to work when some little time for its operation.[6]

Wilberforce confided to his diary his disappointment.

I own it quite lowers my spirits to see all my hopes for this year at once blasted, yet *I can't help myself.* To be sure, one session in such a case as this is not much; yet as we know not what may happen in the interval, I tremble lest some insurrection, or other event with two handles, should turn men against us. Still it is a great reconciler that I can't help myself.[7]

To Lord Muncaster he was more sanguine. He remembered the Lords' opposition to his bills twelve years previously, and was aware he needed to do all he could to maximize the chances of success.

Letter to Muncaster

The more I reflect upon it, the more I am thankful that Providence graciously conducted me to this great cause. We must now exert ourselves. On the next year much depends. The Almighty alone knows what is to be the issue. It was truly humiliating to see, in the House of Lords [in 1792], four of the Royal Family come down to vote against the poor, helpless, friendless Slaves. I sometimes think the Almighty can scarcely suffer us to be rid of such a load of wickedness, to which we cling so fondly, without making us suffer for our bigoted attachment. It is often the way of Heaven to let the error bring its own punishment along with it. Well, my friend, it will one day be consoling, that you and I exerted ourselves to clear the ship of this sinking cargo.[8]

Pitt's Delayed Promise

There was some good news though. Pitt promised to issue a Royal Proclamation (a direct law in the name of the King, not requiring a vote in either House) that would outlaw the slave trade in the new colonies still being acquired in the war with France: 'Called (July 3rd) on Pitt, who positively said he had no doubt of stopping the Trade by Royal Proclamation. Very strong on this, and against any vote of parliament.'[9]

Unfortunately Pitt was now failing in health, and only a shadow of the efficient administrator who had first taken office in 1784. Due to the war, he now delayed any other piece of government business until the last possible

moment. His inaction became a huge frustration to Wilberforce and the rest of the Clapham Sect.

Pitt's Inaction

Let me beg you, my dear Pitt, to have the proclamation
issued for stopping the Guiana supply of slaves. If I felt
less on that subject, I should say more; but I really do
feel on it very deeply, and so I know you would also, if
your attention were not absorbed by such a number of
pressing matters: but it will not cost you half an hour I
hope to settle this. I beg you will remember how much
I myself am personally concerned in it, if any other
excuse be necessary for my boring you so about it than
the merits of the subject itself . . . I repeat it, half an
hour would settle the whole – the forms are at hand in
the Council Office.[10]

Pitt continued to procrastinate, and it was only in September
1805 that the Privy Council finally issued the proclamation.

The 1805 Session

The abolitionists decided their best chance of getting a
bill through the Lords in 1805 was to first again take a bill
through the Commons. If they could do this, and show
that the Commons had for two years decisively spoken for
abolition, they reasoned the Lords would be more likely to
support them. If they did it early enough in the session for
the Lords to have time for a full debate, they were optimistic of success.

   Wilberforce again prepared exhaustively for the coming
debate, and shared research work out amongst Stephen,

Macaulay, Muncaster, a rejuvenated Thomas Clarkson who had returned from the Lake District, and the two young sons of Charles Grant. But in the debate he was disappointed.

Another Crushing Defeat

Second reading of the Abolition Bill. I said nothing at opening, and not enough at the close, but did not expect such an issue. Besides, felt as if I could not go well. Beat, alas, 70 to 77. Sad work! Though I thought we might be hard run from the face of the House, I could not expect the defeat, and all expressed astonishment. The Irish members absent, or even turned against us . . . Great canvassing of our enemies, and several of our friends absent through forgetfulness, or accident, or engagements preferred from lukewarmness.[11]

To the clerk of the Commons Wilberforce put on a brave face.

Continued Optimism

Mr Hatsel (clerk of the House of Commons): 'Mr Wilberforce, you ought not to expect to *carry* a measure of this kind. You have a turn for business, and this is a very creditable employment for you; but you and I have seen enough of life to know that people are not induced to act upon what affects their interests by any abstract arguments.'

Mr Wilberforce: 'Mr Hatsel, I *do* expect to carry it, and what is more, I feel assured I shall carry it speedily. I have observed the gradual change which has been going on in men's minds for some time past, and though the measure may be delayed for a year or two, yet I am convinced that before long it will be accomplished.'[12]

But to his diary, as in the crushing defeats of 1792 and 1796, he shared his real feelings. 'I never felt so much on any parliamentary occasion. I could not sleep after first waking at night. The poor blacks rushed into my mind, and the guilt of our wicked land.'[13] Defeat in the Commons made it impossible to resurrect the 1804 bill in the Lords. The cause was lost again for another year.

Enter Dundas Again

When Pitt returned as Prime Minister he brought back Henry Dundas to his Cabinet. Few doubted Dundas's administrative skill, but he had come under suspicion due to financial irregularities during a previous spell as treasurer of the navy. He had tolerated some of those working for him in taking public money for private ends. The opposition proposed a motion that Dundas resign.

The ensuing debate was finely balanced. Wilberforce entered it not knowing which way to vote. But as he listened to both sides, he found there were no real arguments that explained or exonerated Dundas's conduct. When he finally spoke, he made a devastating case for how Dundas had betrayed the public by allowing such corruption to happen: 'I really cannot find language sufficiently strong to express my utter detestation of such conduct.'[14]

His speech was thought to sway forty MPs. When the result came it was tied at 216 to 216. The speaker, who had a casting vote on such occasions, was said to have visibly turned white. He sought an adjournment for ten minutes, and then finally cast his vote . . . against. Dundas's career was over. Pitt broke down in tears, and was escorted from the chamber by friends as the opposition jeered and cried out 'resign, resign'.

Wilberforce had voted independently rather than along party lines ever since his conversion, and this had been one of his most difficult tests. He voted against his great friend Pitt, and against the man who more than anyone had obstructed the abolition and the East Indian causes in the 1790s, but he did it out of his principle of always voting according to his conscience. He only saw Dundas once more.

Final Meeting with Dundas

We did not meet for a long time, and all his connexions most violently abused me. About a year before he died, we met in the stone passage which leads from the Horse Guards to the Treasury. We came suddenly upon each other, just in the open part, where the light struck upon our faces. We saw one another, and at first I thought he was passing on, but he stopped and called out, 'Ah Wilberforce, how do you do?' and gave me a hearty shake by the hand. I would have given a thousand pounds for that shake. I never saw him afterwards.[15]

Death of Pitt

Pitt's health continued to worsen. The November 1805 victory over Napoleon at the Battle of Trafalgar brought some relief, but even this was accompanied with the tragic death of naval hero Admiral Nelson at the moment of victory. Three weeks later Napoleon won a decisive victory at the Battle of Austerlitz, and Pitt went into decline. He died in January 1806, aged just forty-eight. Despite the differences between them over the previous twelve months, Wilberforce had lost one of his closest and oldest friends.

Wilberforce's Regrets

There is something peculiarly affecting in the time and circumstances of poor Pitt's death. I own I have a thousand times (aye, times without number) wished and hoped that a quiet interval would be afforded him, perhaps in the evening of life, in which he and I might confer freely on the most important of all subjects. But the scene is closed – for ever.[16]

Lord Grenville became Prime Minister, and Charles Fox Foreign Secretary.

Foreign Slave Bill

For the 1806 session the abolition committee tried a new tactic. Rather than bring their standard bill for full abolition, James Stephen suggested a different course that would take out the vast majority of the French and Spanish slave trade, and over 50 per cent of the British trade.

Stephen realized that, due to the Napoleonic wars, much of the slave trade was taking place in ships sailing under neutral flags. The French and Spanish slave ships were flying American flags for fear of attack by the British navy. Stephen suggested a bill that would 1) enable the British navy to search neutral ships, 2) prevent British trade with enemy colonies and 3) prevent British trade with neutral colonies. It sounded patriotic, but it would also have the benefit of cutting down hugely the transatlantic slave trade.

Wilberforce wrote to Grenville, who immediately saw how this could help the war effort and further the abolition cause, whilst also keeping all his government supporters onside. Wilberforce kept silent through the whole debates, pretending it was all a government measure, when in reality the whole thing had been planned by Stephen and himself. The bill passed through both Houses without serious opposition.

Abolition by Stealth

Sunday, 18th [May 1806]. We have carried the Foreign Slave Bill, and we are now deliberating whether we shall push the main question. O Lord, do Thou guide us right, and enable me to maintain a spiritual mind amid all my hurry of worldly business, having my conversation in heaven.[17]

Wilberforce wanted to capitalize on their success with a bill for full abolition that year, but Grenville persuaded him that time was again running short in the parliamentary session, and they would be better off passing a general resolution condemning the trade, to pave the way for full abolition the following year. The government proposed resolutions that the slave trade was 'contrary to the principles of justice, humanity, and sound policy'[18] and that the House would 'with all practicable expedition proceed to take effectual measures for abolishing the said trade'.[19] Wilberforce started to become more optimistic. 'We carried our resolutions 100 and odd to 14, and my address without a division. If it please God to spare the health of Fox, and to keep him and Grenville together, I hope we shall next year see the termination of all our labours.'[20]

Before the close of the session he and Stephen also worked with Fox and Grenville to pass laws preventing non-slave ships from engaging in the trade, stopping a potential late flurry of slave trading before final abolition. That summer he began work on a new book, concisely setting out all the arguments for abolition to the general public he had been advocating in parliament for the past twenty years. 'A pamphlet thrown in just in such circumstances, may be like a shot which hits between wind and water; it might prove of decisive efficiency. It will be well to supply people who wish to come over, with reasons for voting for us.'[21]

The 1807 Session

But Fox was not spared. He died in October 1806, forcing Grenville to call a general election, and sending Wilberforce off to Yorkshire to campaign for his seat. He won again, raced back to London to finish his book, and had it published on 31 January 1807, just four days before an abolition bill was again brought to parliament.

But now there was another change. Grenville had boosted his support through the election, and decided to introduce the abolition bill through the Lords first. Proposing the bill himself as Prime Minister, and fresh from an election victory for his party, the House of Lords for the first time passed a motion to abolish the slave trade, voting 100 to 34. Wilberforce then began the passage of the bill through the Commons.

Victory in Sight

[13 February 1807] An Abolition Committee. Looking at the list of the House of Commons. A terrific list of doubtfuls. Lord Grenville not confident on looking at Abolition list; yet I think we shall carry it too. Several West Indians with us. How popular Abolition is, just now! God can turn the hearts of men.[22]

It passed the first reading in the Commons. Everyone knew the anti-abolitionists would do all they could to oppose it on the second reading. The crucial debate came on 28 February. That night, sensing what was about to happen, speaker after speaker condemned the slave trade, and praised Wilberforce for his efforts in persevering over the past twenty years. It culminated with Samuel Romilly, the Solicitor General, contrasting Wilberforce with Napoleon.

Romilly's Praise

When I look at the man at the head of the French monarchy, surrounded as he is with all the pomp of power, and all the pride of victory, distributing kingdoms to his family, and principalities to his followers, seeming, as he sits upon his throne to have reached the summit of human ambition and the pinnacle of earthly happiness, and when I follow that man into his closet or to his bed, and consider the pangs with which his solitude must be tortured and his repose banished, by the recollection of the blood he has spilled and the oppressions he has committed; and when I compare with those

pangs of remorse the feelings which must accompany
my honourable friend from this house to his home,
after the vote of this night shall have confirmed the
object of his humane and unceasing labours; when he
retires to the bosom of his happy and delighted family,
when he lays himself down on his bed, reflecting on
the innumerable voices that will be raised in every
quarter of the world to bless him, how much more pure
and perfect felicity must he enjoy, in the consciousness
of having preserved so many millions of his fellow-
creatures.[23]

It all became too much for Wilberforce and he started
weeping. The whole House got to their feet to cheer and
clap, giving a unique standing ovation to him in acknowl-
edgement of his tireless campaign. He sat with his head
in his hands, knowing he had finally won. The vote took
place at 5 a.m.

Victory at Last

At length divided, 283 to 16. A good many came over
to Palace Yard after House up, and congratulated me
. . .

Wilberforce: 'Well, Henry, what shall we abolish
next?'
Thornton: 'The lottery, I think.'
William Smith: 'Let us make out the names of these
sixteen miscreants; I have four of them.'
Wilberforce: 'Never mind the miserable 16, let us think
of our glorious 283.'[24]

The scale of the victory was incredible, but it immediately made the abolition committee press further and obtain penalty clauses for any who continued the slave trade. Wilberforce brought in Stephen to draft the clauses with the government lawyers.

Letter to Stephen

We agreed that the division of last night has quite changed the state of things, and that it is highly desirable now to put in the penalties [for non-compliance]. It was settled to send the clauses to Vivian, and to desire you and him to meet and talk them over together.

The bill passed its third reading in both Commons and Lords without mishap, and was signed into law on 25 May. Ironically this became the last act of the Grenville government, which had tried to force Catholic emancipation on George III, but found him as inflexible on the subject as Pitt had found him seven years previously. The government collapsed ... but the Slave Trade Act 1807 had been passed. Wilberforce was ecstatic, and through all the acclaim he recognized God as the one due the real praise. 'Oh what thanks do I owe the Giver of all good, for bringing me in His gracious providence to this great cause, which at length, after almost nineteen years' labour, is successful!'[26] 'God will bless this country. The first authentic account of the defeat of the French has come to-day.'[27]

Yorkshire Elections

Spencer Perceval was appointed Prime Minister, and immediately called fresh elections. For the first time in decades, a full ballot was held across Yorkshire rather than the usual system of hustings.

The expense was huge – more even than Wilberforce could afford. But now his popularity resulted in people across the country subscribing money to pay his expenses. £18,000 was contributed by Yorkshire supporters in the first week, and by the end of the campaign £64,455 had been received in total from across Britain. Wilberforce retained his seat, despite spending a tenth of what his two opponents spent combined. Many voters refused to accept the customary payment to vote for him, and after the campaign 46 per cent of the subscription money was returned.

Magnanimity in Victory

Surely it calls for deep humiliation, and warm acknowledgment, that God has given me favour with men, that after guiding me by His providence to that great cause, He crowned my efforts with success, and obtained for me so much good-will and credit. Alas, Thou knowest, Lord, all my failings, errors, infirmities, and negligencies in relation to this great cause; but Thou art all goodness and forbearance towards me.[28]

The country had vindicated his long campaign, and he was the most popular politician in the nation. With the slave trade abolished, the government even now took over the role of managing Sierra Leone, saving himself, Thornton and the rest of the Clapham Sect another of the costly burdens they had taken on. By summer 1807 he could pray, 'O Lord, direct me to some new line of usefulness, for Thy glory, and the good of my fellow-creatures.'[29]

West Indian Abolition

Key Learning Points

Spiritual Formation

Don't judge on personal bias. Treat every issue independently, on the facts at hand.

Forgive. Wilberforce didn't bear grudges despite all the times Dundas had opposed him. 'I would have given a thousand pounds for that shake.'

Remain humble in success. Recognize God's hand in bringing any success you experience.

Be magnanimous in victory. 'Never mind the miserable 16, let us think of our glorious 283.'

Discerning Vision

Seek God after success. When the vision is completed, seek him for what thing you should be working towards next.

Leadership Skills

Don't take your eye off the ball. The 100 Irish MPs added four years previously were a missed opportunity. Had Wilberforce brought abolition bills during this time, the slave trade might have ended earlier.

Don't be afraid of the 'big ask'. Find the right person for important jobs. Grenville had to be approached to take the bill through the Lords. His leadership and involvement made all the difference.

Match the vision with people's interests. The Foreign Slave Bill appealed to the British national interest during war time. But it also abolished much of the slave trade, making it easier for parliament to ban the trade outright the following year.

Persevere. Some victories only come after long and costly battles.

Press home your advantage. When your influence is highest, push forward. The abolitionists saw the huge scale of their victory, so pressed for penalty clauses in the bill.

Mission Skills

 Don't delay in talking with people about God. Wilberforce always regretted not talking more seriously with Pitt about Christianity.

Agitate on the ground. In campaigning, the grass roots need to be agitating for change to make the politicians listen. The MPs only passed abolition because they saw from the petitions how much the general population wanted the slave trade abolished.

East Indian Victory: 1807–1813

After twenty years' wait, Wilberforce seized the opportunity of the renewal of the East India Charter to insert clauses sending missionaries to the subcontinent. His battle over the slave trade meant he knew how to lead a campaign to victory.

East India Campaign

With the slave trade abolished, and the East India Charter almost up for renewal after twenty years, the Clapham Sect began to think through how they could reverse the 1793 defeat over sending missionaries. Wilberforce was convinced this was the next pressing issue.

Importance of the India Cause

To me, I frankly declare that our suffering our East India subjects, nay tenants, for such they are, to remain, without an effort to the contrary, under the most depraving and cruel system of superstition which ever enslaved a people, is, considering all our own blessings . . . the greatest by far, now that the Slave Trade has ceased, of all the national crimes by which we are provoking the vengeance and suffering the chastisement of Heaven.[1]

But before the 1813 campaign and debates, there would be a significant change for the Clapham community.

Leaving Clapham

Wilberforce had for some time contemplated moving away from Clapham. He knew he needed to spend less time at his Westminster home opposite parliament in order to find more solitude. As early as 1805 he had considered a move.

Needing More Solitude

This living in Palace Yard is destructive to my time . . . A residence near London would withdraw me from company, and give me more time. Yet I dread the separation which my leaving Broomfield would make from my chief friends, the Thorntons, Teignmouths, Stephens, Venn, Macaulay, with whom I now live like a brother.[2]

But now he also considered moving out of Clapham. His old friend Isaac Milner had previously warned him of 'a danger in living altogether at Clapham – danger of conceit and spiritual pride, and a cold, critical spirit. He imputes this less to me than to some others – but the danger is great.'[3] Wilberforce took this on board. But it was his family that was the clinching argument.

By 1808 he and Barbara had six children: William (born in 1798), Barbara (1799), Elizabeth (1801), Robert (1802), Samuel (1805) and Henry (1807). At home in the garden at Clapham he had picked up baby Henry, causing Henry to promptly burst into tears. His nanny explained to Wilberforce, 'He always is afraid of strangers.'[4]

Wilberforce was mortified, and resolved to move somewhere he could spend more time with his family and less time in company. He sold both Broomfield and Old Palace Yard to Thornton, and in November 1808 took a house in Kensington Gore, where the Royal Albert Hall now stands. Downsizing from two houses to one would save him five or six hundred pounds a year, and he could still live at Old Palace Yard during parliamentary sessions as a tenant of the ever-generous Thornton. He also bought the neighbouring cottage to his new house and turned it into his office. Working there he could remain uninterrupted, whilst callers at the main house could be honestly told by the servants that 'Mr Wilberforce was not at home.' He called his office the Nuisance, and it served him well during all his time at Kensington, as did the larger house. 'I am almost ashamed of the handsomeness of my house, my verandah, &c . . . I am almost uneasy about my house and furniture, lest I am spending too much money upon it, so as to curtail my charities.'[5]

The house saved expense, plus gave him more time for solitude and his children. Stephen soon moved to be close to him, and the other members of the Clapham Sect remained regular visitors, but overall he got more quality time with his family.

Family Time

[June 1810] Playing at cricket with Mr Babington, a ball struck my foot with great violence, and . . . by the positive injunctions of my surgeon, I have been ever since sentenced to a sofa. It will lessen the marvel, and render the tale less laughable, to hear that my son William was the main personage in the dramatis personae of the cricket players, and I have not played with him at cricket before, for I know not how long.[6]

Sundays with His Family

Sundays especially were a family day together, when all talk of politics and campaigning was put aside, in favour of church, rest and quality time. Only close friends were allowed to join in these family days. He did occasionally break his Sabbath rule to prepare for a crucial political debate, but these things occurred only a couple of times a decade.

Harford's Recollection of Wilberforce

High value for the house of God, and the hours of secret meditation . . . made his Sundays cool down his mind, and allay the rising fever of political excitement. Sunday turned all his feelings into a new channel. His letters were put aside, and all thoughts of business banished.[7]

Wilberforce became such a believer in the importance of Sunday as a day of rest that he even petitioned Prime

Minister Perceval, himself an evangelical Christian, to move the opening day of parliament from a Monday, since this would cause MPs from across the country to travel down to London on the Sunday before.

A Sabbath Campaigner

Dear Wilberforce,
You will be glad to hear that it is determined to postpone the meeting of parliament till Thursday the 19th, instead of the Monday the 16th, to obviate the objections which you have suggested to the meeting on that day.
Yours very truly,
Spencer Perceval.[8]

Abolition Matters

During week-days he continued to be occupied by abolition matters. The first immediate task was to ensure the British enforced the slave trade ban they had passed in 1807; to this end he persuaded parliament in 1808 to set up a naval squadron to police the seas off West Africa and prevent British slave ships from operating.

The second task was to persuade other nations to give up the trade. Wilberforce constantly wrote to foreign ambassadors, and whoever was current Foreign Secretary, to entreat France, Spain, Portugal and the United States to give up the trade.

1808 Letter to US President Thomas Jefferson

A compact formed between our two countries for the benevolent purpose of stopping, perhaps, the most destructive scourge that ever afflicted the human race, may lead to similar agreements with other countries, until at length all the civilized nations of the earth shall have come into this concert of benevolence.

But his frequent lobbying on the issue still wasn't enough for the passionate Stephen, who saw that Wilberforce was also constantly distracted by other matters. Yorkshire constituents and people seeking his advice, his connections or his fortune constantly thronged the house at Kensington Gore. Ever the honest man, Stephen wrote with his plain criticism.

Letter from James Stephen

My dear Wilberforce,
I send for your consideration a paper that may serve to show you how absolutely necessary it is you should resolutely make time to think and act on Abolition matters . . . If better and clearer heads, and more disengaged hands, than mine, do not lead in this cause; and if you, who *must* be the public leader, are to be only a battering-ram to be pushed forward, instead of a fore-horse in the team to pull as well as guide the rest, the cause is lost, the Abolition is undone. It will sink under the weight of your daily epistles; your post privilege will be the bondage of Africa, and your covers the

funereal pyre of her new-born hopes. Millions will sigh in hopeless wretchedness, that Wilberforce's correspondents may not think him uncivil or unkind . . . But it is vain to complain. So things will continue, I know, and it is only making bad worse to take up your time with long expostulations. Read, however, and send me back my paper.[10]

Quitting Yorkshire

Stephen also advised Wilberforce to give up his Yorkshire seat for a smaller constituency. If he took a rotten borough with no obligation to serve his electors, he could devote more time to speaking out on the important matters in the House, where his prestige and experience now gave him a powerful voice. Wilberforce wrestled with the pros and cons of the situation, especially about how a smaller constituency could help him with his goal of spending more time with his family. He had been offered the seat of Bramber, a Sussex coastal town.

Main Reasons for Quitting Yorkshire Seat

The state of my family – my eldest son just turned thirteen, and three other boys, and two girls. Now though I should commit the learning of my boys to others, yet the moral part of education should be greatly carried on by myself. They claim a father's heart, eye, and voice, and friendly intercourse. Now so long as I am M. P. for Yorkshire, it will, I fear, be impossible for me to give my heart and time to the work as I ought, unless I become a negligent M. P. such as does not become our great county. I even doubt whether I ought not to quit public life altogether, on the ground that if I remain in the House even for Bramber, which Lord Calthorpe kindly offers, I shall still be so much of a political man, that the work of education will not be set to heartily.[11]

He also felt he was becoming too forgetful and too old to faithfully represent so large a constituency. He consulted the Clapham Sect, but was 'much embarrassed by the conflicting advice of friends – Babington strong for absolute retiring – Stephen and others for giving up Yorkshire – but Grant and Henry Thornton against my quitting the county'.[12] Eventually he decided to quit Yorkshire and take Bramber at the 1812 election.

It was also for health he stood down. In December 1811 he was severely ill for many weeks; he became so frail his chin would droop onto his chest, and his voice became hoarse. He still had frequent stomach upsets, and had been taking opium every day now for over twenty years. By early 1812 he complained, 'I am wanting my voice much, that I may plead the cause of Christianity in India.'[13]

The India Missionary Cause

The Clapham Sect knew that to overcome the East Indian lobby and persuade parliament of the importance of the missionary cause in India they would need more than just eloquence in the Commons. They began with Wilberforce persuading the Prime Minister of the importance of the issue: 'Went to see him entirely about the East India charter occasion, for securing the means of introducing Christian light into India. He freely professed himself favourable to the object, but saw great difficulties in the way, and asked for some distinct proposition.'[14]

They next used the *Christian Observer* to begin raising the conditions of India in the minds of the public. And in April 1812 they obtained a commitment from the Church Missionary Society towards sending missionaries to India. Things seemed to be moving well, but then disaster struck. On 11 May 1812 Spencer Perceval was assassinated in the central lobby of the Houses of Parliament, shot by a trader who had lost money due to the Royal Proclamation outlawing the slave trade to the West Indian colonies acquired during the war. Stephen had become close friends with Perceval due to the Prime Minister's steadfast support for abolition, and had even taken a seat in parliament to help defend the Proclamation in Commons debates. He was devastated by the killing, but a few days later went to visit the assassin in prison, entreating him to repent before he was executed. Wilberforce was intensely proud of his friend and brother-in-law. 'Oh wonderful power of Christianity.'[15]

Other Pursuits

Throughout the focus on India, Wilberforce had other pursuits too. He closely followed the Commons debates on votes for Roman Catholics. Wilberforce was one of the few evangelicals to realize the prejudice many felt against Catholicism, and was determined to vote for the rights of Irish Catholics, despite the unpopularity it would bring to him.

Irish Catholic Rights

Lord, direct me, all the religious people are on the other side, but they are sadly prejudiced . . . It grieves me to separate from the Dean [Milner], and all my religious friends; but conscience must be obeyed. God does not direct us to use carnal weapons in His cause.[16]

East India Campaign

But the India cause consumed most of his time. The Clapham Sect now called on the abolition network around the country to petition parliament on behalf of the Indian people. They shared stories of the brutality of the Indian caste system; how under Hinduism it was commonplace for widows to be burned alive on the funeral pyres of their husbands in a practice known as suttee; how babies were killed as a form of birth control; how human sacrifice was common in the worship of certain Indian deities. They used shocking stories to call on the British people to call on parliament to stop these atrocities, and make provision for humane laws and education to be introduced to India. Wilberforce wrote to Hannah More asking for a petition from Bristol: 'You know enough of life to be aware that in parliamentary measures of importance, more is to be done out of the House than in it.'[17]

Letter to Hannah More

You will agree with me, that now the Slave Trade is abolished, this is by far the greatest of our national sins

> . . . But all this is to lead you to stir up a petition in Bristol, and any other place. The petitions for abolishing the Slave Trade were very general, and very useful; why not on this occasion also?[18]

More succeeded in getting a petition from Bristol, and called on some of her own friends to send one from Manchester. The whole country was mobilized; parliament eventually received 837 petitions on the subject, signed by over one million people. It was more even than had sent petitions on the slave trade, but it was needed. Wilberforce observed, 'Nine out of ten of the witnesses who will be called to give evidence are hostile to us. The House of Commons in general is disposed against us, and the newspapers are still more hostile to us than the House.'[19]

The Clapham Sect worked on two levels, mobilizing the country at large, but also maintaining their talks with the government: 'moving for many East India papers, talked over the mode of proceeding in the question in cabinet council with Grant, Babington, Stephen, and Henry Thornton'.[20] When the new charter finally was presented to parliament, they had worked with Foreign Secretary Castlereagh to include all the clauses they wanted, supporting the provisions of education and missionary work.

A Charter Written in Clapham

Lord Castlereagh agreed to Lord Buckingamshire's and our arrangement for East India Christianizing

Resolutions – far surpassing my expectations . . . Let me express my humiliation, and my gratitude to God, for enabling us to agree with government as to the conditions for sending out missionaries, and in general as to improving, moralizing, and Christianizing India. I humbly hope that God has great designs in view for the East, and that they will be executed by Great Britain.[21]

The charter now needed to receive parliamentary approval, and Wilberforce needed to defend the clauses he had inserted. The opening debate happened on 22 June 1813.

The East India Company Debate

It was late when I got up; but by divine grace I was enabled to speak for two hours, (though curtailing from fear of being tedious,) and with great acceptance. I spoke better than of late, Bankes kindly said to me, I had got into my old vein, and though the matter was unpopular, yet admirably heard. Only a little afterwards from opponents, and we carried it, about 89 to 36, beyond all hope. I heard afterwards that many good men had been praying for us all night.[22]

Wilberforce's speech contained forceful damnations of the Indian caste system, of infanticide, of suttee and of human sacrifice, and gave his reasoning for why Christianity and education were the best solutions to cure these ills.

Excerpts from Wilberforce's Speech

That remedy, Sir, is Christianity . . . On the very first promulgation of Christianity, it was declared by its great Author, as 'glad tidings to the poor'; and, ever faithful to her character, Christianity still delights to instruct the ignorant, to succour the needy, to comfort the sorrowful, to visit the forsaken . . .

Why need I, in this country, insist on the evils which arise merely out of the institution of Caste itself . . . Even where slavery has existed, it has commonly been possible (though in the West Indies, alas! artificial difficulties have been interposed) for individuals to burst their bonds, and assert the privileges of their nature. But the more cruel shackles of Caste are never to be shaken; as well might a dog, or any other of the brute creation . . . aspire to the dignity and rights of man . . .

Again in India we find prevalent that evil, I mean infanticide, against which we might have hoped that nature herself would have supplied adequate restraints . . .

Another practice . . . has increased since the country came under our dominion. Great pains were taken by the missionaries a few years ago to ascertain the number of widows which were annually burnt in a district thirty miles round Calcutta, and the House will be astonished to hear that in this comparatively small area 130 widows were burnt in six months. In the year 1803 within the same space the number amounted to 275, one of whom was a girl of eleven years of age. I ought to state that the utmost pains were taken to have the account correct; certain persons were employed purposely to watch and report the number of these horrible exhibitions; and the place, person, and other particulars were regularly certified. After hearing this you will not be surprised on being told that the whole number of these annual sacrifices of women who are often thus cruelly torn from their children at the very time when from the loss of their father they must be in the greatest need of the fostering care of the surviving parent, is estimated, I think, in the Bengal provinces, to be 10,000 . . .

And now, Sir . . . I allude to the various obscene and bloody rites of their idolatrous ceremonies, with all their unutterable abominations . . . Dr Carey, the missionary, has calculated, that, taking in all the various modes and forms of destruction connected with the worship at the temple of Jaggernaut in Orissa, the lives of 100,000 human beings are annually expended in the service of that single idol.[23]

At the next reading the Anglo Indian lobby tried to remove the clauses, arguing Wilberforce was trying to compel Indians to become Christians. He was doing nothing of the sort: 'Compulsion and Christianity! Why, the very terms are at variance with each other: the ideas are incompatible.'[24] He was simply pleading for Christian missionaries to be allowed to enter India, where they would do far more to promote Indian education and fight against these injustices than the East India Company had done. The Company lobby was outvoted. It was now legal to be a Christian missionary in British controlled India, and it was legal to provide education for the Indians. Wilberforce and his friends had again achieved what before seemed impossible.

Victory for Indian Education

The East India Bill passed, and the missionary, or rather the Christian, cause fought through, without division, to the last. We were often alarmed. Lord Castlereagh has managed it admirably – coolly and quietly. The petitions, of which a greater number than were ever known, have carried our question instrumentally, the good providence of God really.[25]

A chance for a better relationship between Britain and India had been created. Missionaries began setting up schools, and the East India Company realized it could no longer ignore the practice of suttee. 'I am persuaded that we have, by our success in that instance, laid the foundation stone of the grandest edifice that ever was raised in Asia.'[26]

East Indian Victory

Key Learning Points

Spiritual Formation

Prioritize your family. Your role as a parent or a spouse is the most important role you can ever be called to.

Don't lie. Even white lies should be avoided. Wilberforce took the Nuisance so he could work without being disturbed without having to ask his servant to lie for him.

Stand against prejudice. Stand up for what is right, even when that means opposing your own friends.

Recognize your frailty. Give up some responsibilities when you can no longer complete them as well as others could.

Discerning Vision

Focus on your calling. Be generous to other people and causes, but don't be distracted from the things God has called you to.

Mission Skills

Work on two levels in campaigns. Create a mass movement to pressurize those in power, but also work with those in power to lead them through change

An International Campaigner: 1813–1821

The final decade of Wilberforce's public life was spent trying to achieve international slave trade abolition, trying to improve the conditions of slaves in the West Indies, and then finally looking towards the eradication of slavery itself.

Wilberforce was now aged fifty-four, but had lost none of his self-criticism when judging his spiritual state.

Self-Judgment for Spiritual Growth

I must secure more time for private devotion, for self-examination, for meditation, for keeping the heart, and even doing the duties of life, or the most pressing claims will carry it, not the strongest. I have been living far too publicly for me . . . Lord, help me. The shortening of private devotions starves the soul, it grows lean and faint. This must not be. Oh how sad, that after trying to lead a Christian life for twenty-eight years, I should be at all staggered by worldly company.[1]

International Abolition Part One

His most pressing work now was to continue pushing other major powers to give up the slave trade. In April 1814 there was a breakthrough. Napoleon was defeated by a coalition involving Britain, Spain, Portugal and much of the rest of Europe. After twenty-one years of near constant warfare, it seemed peace could return to Europe. The settlement talks involved all the major European powers, so were an opportunity for an international conference on the slave trade, much as Wilberforce had been advocating for years. He wrote to Russian Tsar Alexander and French Foreign Minister Talleyrand to persuade them of the cause, and the abolition committee sent Macaulay off to Paris to attend the provisional peace talks.

But hopes for immediate international abolition were dashed. Britain agreed to hand back all of France's colonies, and permitted them to continue the slave trade for a further five years. Castlereagh returned to London to a great reception as the arbiter of European peace, except from Wilberforce. 'I cannot but conceive that I behold in his hand the death-warrant of a multitude of innocent victims, men, women, and children, whom I had fondly indulged the hope of having myself rescued from destruction.'[2]

Many of the European leaders came to London in the coming months, and Wilberforce talked with whoever he could to further abolition, including the King of Prussia and the Polish Prince. Tsar Alexander revealed that Castlereagh had not pressed for abolition at the Paris peace talks.

Tsar Alexander

He took me by the hand, very cordially, and assured me that he was much interested for my object, and very glad to see me . . . When I was expressing my concern about the treaty, he said, 'What could be done, when your own ambassador gave way?'[3]

Wilberforce resorted to his technique of asking for petitions, and again over 800 arrived, this time requiring the British Foreign Secretary to be more firm on abolition when the final peace negotiations took place in Vienna. Wilberforce also ensured that Castlereagh be fully prepared with the necessary arguments by bringing in Macaulay to brief him.

Request to Macaulay

You will concur with me that it may be well to furnish Lord Castlereagh with short notes like a lawyer's brief, of all the main propositions on which the case of Abolition rests, or rather I mean of all the facts. For having been our opponent, he never, depend on it, admitted into his mind any of these considerations which were so firmly established in ours.[4]

Castlereagh went to the Vienna peace talks not only with Macaulay's notes, but with several copies of Wilberforce's 1807 book on slavery to distribute.

Letter from Henry Thornton to Hannah More

We have seen much of Wilberforce, and heard his letters from many of the renowned of the earth, all seeming to pay homage to him. Lord Castlereagh tells him that he has obeyed his commands, and put his book into the hands of each of the Sovereigns . . . the name of Wilberforce has attained new celebrity, and his character and general opinions a degree of weight, which perhaps no private individual not invested with office ever possessed.[5]

The Congress of Vienna was disrupted by the return of Napoleon, and a further hundred days of his rule, finally ending in the Battle of Waterloo. But when Napoleon returned he outlawed the slave trade across all French territories. When he was defeated at Waterloo, the French government decided to uphold the ban.

Letter from Castlereagh

I have the gratification of acquainting you that the long desired object is accomplished, and that the present messenger carries to Lord Liverpool the unqualified and total Abolition of the Slave Trade throughout the dominions of France.[6]

Now France had joined Britain, Denmark and the United States in banning the trade. The international campaigning was slowly bearing fruit.

But tragedy also came. In early 1815 Henry Thornton died from tuberculosis. He had been Wilberforce's closest friend, house-mate and co-worker for over twenty years. Wilberforce was stunned. He wrote to Macaulay, 'I seem to love my own and our dear Henry's surviving friends better since his being taken away from us.'[7]

Register Bill

There was still work for the Clapham Sect though. Despite their best hopes, the 1807 abolition had not brought any improvement to the barbaric conditions most slaves in the West Indies had to endure. This had always been the hope of the abolitionists. Said Wilberforce, 'Our grand object, and our universal language was and is, to produce by Abolition a disposition to breed instead of buying. This is the great vital principle which would work in every direction, and produce reform everywhere.'[8]

Since conditions hadn't improved they needed to do something else. Stephen advocated creating a registry system, where all plantations kept detailed records of the slaves they held. This would make it harder for plantation owners to maim and murder slaves in the way they currently did, or to smuggle in new slaves. He and Wilberforce got the government to agree to a Registry Bill, but it was continually deferred.

The ever passionate Stephen became incensed, and threatened to resign his parliamentary seat in protest. 'If Lord Castlereagh fails to redeem this pledge, may God not spare me, if I spare the noble Lord and his colleagues.'[9] For Stephen, nothing could excuse anyone who couldn't see West Indian slavery for the evil system it was. 'I would rather be on friendly terms with a man who had strangled my infant son than support an administration guilty of slackness in suppressing the slave trade.'[10]

Wilberforce persuaded Stephen to keep his seat, since he could be of more use in parliament than out of it. But he also wrote to the Prime Minister about his frustrations on the delays.

Letter to Prime Minister Lord Liverpool

It really would, on all accounts, grieve me to find myself opposed to your Lordship's government on these great questions of the deepest interest to every man of religion as well as humanity. Hitherto I have abstained from bringing into notice the miseries of the black population, and I would still abstain, if without divulging them they might gradually be removed; but life is wearing away, and I should indeed be sorry if mine were to terminate before at least a foundation had been laid of a system of reformation, which I verily believe would scarcely be more for the comfort of the slaves and free coloured population than it would be for the ultimate security of the West India colonies themselves.[11]

On 5 July 1815 Wilberforce introduced a Registry Bill himself since no one from the government wanted to take on the cause. It encountered strong opposition from the West Indian faction and ran out of time that parliamentary session. Stephen finally did resign his seat in protest.

Wilberforce tried again in 1816 but still couldn't get it through. A slave insurrection was taking place in Barbados, and was blamed on the Abolitionists. Wilberforce believed treating the slaves on the plantations better would lead to less slave revolts, but parliament believed otherwise. He would have tried again in 1817, but decided the time wasn't right to bring up the matter.

Letter to Macaulay

I have for some time been unwillingly yielding to a secret suggestion that it would be better perhaps to lie upon our oars in the Registry Bill, and West Indian cause. When parliament meets, the whole nation, depend upon it, will be looking up for relief from its own burthens, and it would betray an ignorance of all tact to talk to them in such circumstances of the sufferings of the slaves in the West Indies. We should specially guard against appearing to have a world of our own, and to have little sympathy with the sufferings of our countrymen.[12]

Ironically this is exactly how many later historians judged him, due to his support for Pitt's Seditious Assemblies Bill and other curtailments on freedom of speech during the 1790s. By 1818 for the first time he started seriously considering emancipation for all slaves as the only way of improving the West Indies.

Personal Concerns

Throughout this period he was growing more concerned for the future of his children. His eldest son William had started university, but when Wilberforce heard about his licentious lifestyle he was recalled from Cambridge and sent back home. Wilberforce's greatest cause at this time was arguably to see all his children find the same relationship with God that had so changed his own life over thirty years previously.

Concern for His Son

I am anxious to see in you decisive marks of this great change. I come again and again to look and see if it be indeed begun, just as a gardener walks up again and again to examine his fruit trees, and see if his peaches are set, and if they are swelling and becoming larger; finally, if they are becoming ripe and rosy.[13]

William junior married in 1820, and his parents hoped this would lead to him settling down in life. But through all these struggles, Wilberforce determined to remain humble and grateful for all that God had given to him. He devoted an entry in his diary to listing all the reasons and causes he had for humility and gratitude.

Motives for Gratitude

- Born in the eighteenth century, and in England, when the increased wealth and civilization have enabled me to enjoy so many accommodations necessary to my usefulness, much more to my comfort.
- Blessed with acceptance, early and continued, both in public and private life. Raised to so very honourable a station as M. P. for Yorkshire, and enabled to retain it near thirty years, (elected five times, and no prospect of opposition when voluntarily resigned it,) though from considerations weighed in God's sight I neglected all the usual attentions to the county both generally and individually.

- Providentially directed to such a pursuit as Abolition, and blessed by success.
- So many friends, and these so good in themselves, and so kind to me. Scarcely any one so richly provided with kind friends. This is a cause for continual gratitude.
- My domestic blessings. How few who marry so late in life have such affectionate wives! My children all kind and loving to me.
- Above all, my spiritual blessings; having been called, I humbly trust, and drawn by the Holy Spirit, and enlightened, and softened, and in some degree sanctified. It is, I trust, my fixed resolution to desire to please God in all things, and to devote all I have and am to his glory, through Christ and by the Holy Spirit; yet, alas, how little have I of late been living a life of communion with God, in faith, and hope, and love, and joy, and usefulness! God be merciful to me a sinner.[14]

International Abolition Part Two

He was finding greater reasons for gratitude, too, through the progress of the international abolition cause. By 1820 Spain had finally agreed to stop the slave trade, leaving only Portugal as the major power still engaged in it.

Spanish Abolition

A very friendly and handsome letter from Castlereagh informs me, that he has actually received the treaty with Spain (signed) for abolishing the Slave Trade generally and finally in May, 1820, and immediately to the north of the Line. Also, which is scarcely less valuable, that a system of mutual search is agreed to be established for enforcing the Abolition law. Well may we praise God.[15]

His international work led to him not only campaigning for abolition, but also working to support states that were trying to survive in a post-slavery world. Haiti's revolution had transformed the island into a new kingdom ruled by King Henri Christophe. Wilberforce corresponded with Christophe, and sent him missionaries and educators to help the fledgling nation.

Christophe of Haiti

He has requested me to get for him seven schoolmasters, a tutor for his son, and seven different professors for a Royal College he desires to found. Amongst these are a classical professor, a medical, a surgical, a mathematical, and a pharmaceutical chemist.[16]

Other Reform Activities

Wilberforce was always interested in all forms of reform and improvement related to social conditions, whether at home or abroad. He visited Newgate prison with

Elizabeth Fry to see the improvements she had brought there, and became impressed with her brother-in-law Thomas Fowell Buxton, a young evangelical MP who showed great dedication to a number of worthy causes.

Prison Reform

Went with our party to meet Mrs Fry at Newgate. The order she has produced is wonderful – a very interesting visit – much talk with the governor and chaplain – Mrs Fry prayed in recitative – the place from its construction bad.[17]

31st [March 1818]. Much impressed by Mr Buxton's book on our prisons, and the account of Newgate reform. What lessons are taught by Mrs Fry's success! I am still warmed by the account. Were I young, I should instantly give notice of the business, if no one else did.[18]

Queen Caroline Affair

But rather than reform, Wilberforce now became embroiled with issues surrounding the royal family. He had not been on terms with many of them for years; his opposition to the war with France and their vocal support of the slave trade had caused a breach. But that was now in the past. Due to George III's madness, his eldest son was now Prince Regent, and Wilberforce had mixed with him a little on a recent holiday in Brighton: 'When there, the Prince and Duke of Clarence too very civil.'

Brighton Encounters with the Prince Regent

At the Pavilion – the Prince came up to me and reminded me of my singing at the Duchess of Devonshire's ball in 1782, of the particular song, and of our then first knowing each other. 'We are both I trust much altered since, sir.' 'Yes, the time which has gone by must have made a great alteration in us.' 'Something better than that too, I trust, sir.' He then asked me to dine with him the next day, assuring me that I should hear nothing in his house to give me pain.[20]

In 1820 George III died, and the Prince Regent became King. His estranged wife Caroline came back from Europe to be recognized as Queen. George IV detested his wife; after just nine months together and the birth of their daughter they had separated. Now Caroline had returned, but rather than accept his wife back, the King made plans to divorce her.

With the Queen refusing to agree that she had committed adultery, the King planned to pass a bill through parliament proclaiming her guilt. In effect the Lords and the Commons would become divorce courts, determining where the blame lay for the breakdown of the marriage. Wilberforce feared that revelations of adultery (numerous on the King's side) would create a national scandal. The Queen was becoming popular due to the unpopularity of George IV. There was a real danger she could become a figurehead for a whole range of anti-establishment feeling.

A National Scandal

Sunday. I fear lest it should please God to scourge the nation through the medium of this rupture between the King and Queen. If the soldiery should take up her cause, who knows what may happen – and is it very improbable? O Lord, deliver us![21]

The Queen's lawyer was his fellow abolitionist Henry Brougham. Together they agreed a compromise where Caroline could still be called Queen and given a salary by parliament, but would live abroad in Europe, and would not be prayed for in Anglican churches across the country in the weekly prayers for the royal family. Brougham agreed to the plan on behalf of the Queen, and Wilberforce agreed to bring the solution to parliament. He wrote to Macaulay, 'I hope I am averting a great evil.'[22]

The next day Wilberforce led a delegation to the Queen to present the proposal to her. With Brougham stood at her side, she rejected it outright. The press and public had no knowledge of Brougham's prior acceptance on the Queen's behalf, and so thought Wilberforce to be merely an interfering busybody, rather than an honest broker of something previously agreed.

Wilberforce's Unpopularity

I got the nineteen Sunday newspapers once for all the other day, that I might the better judge of their contents; and assuredly such a collection of ribaldry and profaneness never before disgraced my library, and I trust never will again. Of course many of the writers honour me with a peculiar share of attention. But this will soon blow over, and by and by all the well-disposed part of the community will do me justice, and above all, *the Lord will protect.*[23]

The divorce bill was brought in the Lords, and finally passed there, but then dropped in the Commons. The whole episode had discredited the royal family, discredited Wilberforce in the eyes of the country, set back further the anti-slavery cause, and left Wilberforce with a desire to finally quit politics.

Fallout from Caroline Affair

I am doubtful about moving an Address on the Slave Trade. I greatly doubt the wisdom of bringing on these questions now, because the public mind is engrossed with the Queen's business, and because I am unpopular out of doors, though not in the House. What a lesson it is to a man not to set his heart on low popularity, when after forty years' disinterested public service I am believed to be a perfect rascal! Oh what a comfort it is to have to fly for refuge to a God of unchangeable truth and love![24]

I should greatly like to lay a foundation for some future measures for the emancipation of the poor slaves . . . [This] being done, how gladly should I retire! I am quite sick of the wear and tear of the House of Commons; of the envy, malice, and all uncharitableness.[25]

An International Campaigner

Key Learning Points

Spiritual Formation

Be honest with yourself. Sometimes you need to be harsh on yourself, and sometimes you need to be gracious. Always be more honest with yourself than you expect others to be.

Have an attitude of gratitude. One of the best ways to remain grateful is to regularly list all the reasons you have to count your blessings.

Speak out for what is right. Even if you are the only one, and even if this makes you unpopular. Wilberforce criticized the initial peace settlement with France since it allowed for five more years of slave trading to take place.

Don't worry about reputation. 'The Lord will protect.'

Discerning Vision

Prioritize. You cannot achieve everything – what will you focus on?

Mission Skills

Pray for others. Pray for your children, your family and your close friends to come to Christ.

Free At Last: 1821–1833

Wilberforce ended his career campaigning for the end of slavery. In his retirement he remained grateful to God, despite losing his health, his fortune and both his daughters. He died at the same time as slavery died throughout the British Empire.

Thinking of Retirement

By the 1821 parliamentary session Wilberforce was beginning to think of retirement. He was now sixty-two, had been in parliament for over forty years, and recognized others were making speeches far better than his own.

1821 Session

Feb. 21st [1821]. I rather prepared for the coming debate; yet, as too common with me, expended nearly all my time over old accounts, which had only general reference to the subject, and made some little deposits of useful facts, but little or no immediate preparation. My secretary too late. It is sad business to have my eyes in another person's keeping.[1]

> May 25th [1821]. Buxton's capital speech on the crimi-
> nal laws, two hours and forty minutes – nobody tired
> – all information and sense.[2]

> June 20th [1821]. I moved my address on the Aboli-
> tion, urging government to press the matter on foreign
> powers. Mackintosh spoke capitally; I did not at all
> please myself.[3]

His eyesight, which had always been poor, was slowly
getting worse. His small frame often seemed bent double
due to curvature of the spine, and his general health was
poor. He still kept up a rich correspondence with various
world leaders to push forward abolition matters, but was
having to become more reliant on help from others.

Declining Eyesight

> For four or five days I have scarcely been able to look at
> my notes, or make progress in my letter to the Emperor.
> It is vexatious beyond measure to have my time
> frittered away, but my eyes are the chief hindrance. Oh
> that I were young and strong, then I might get up at
> five o'clock in the morning.[4]

Domestic Changes

After thirteen years at Kensington Gore he moved house
to a country retreat called Marden Park, where he could
begin to contemplate retirement. That winter tragedy again
came, when his eldest daughter Barbara died of tuberculosis aged just twenty-two. Wilberforce had to miss the

funeral due to the severe cold weather and his own bad health. He had previously lost friends who attended the cold funerals of others and died as a consequence. Missing the service, he used the time to pray, and once again write down a list of all the reasons he had to be grateful.

Reflections on Daughter Barbara's Death

I went and saw the coffin. How vain the plumes, &c. when the occasion is considered, and the real state of humiliation to which the body is reduced! I must elsewhere note down the mercies and loving-kindnesses of our God and Saviour in this dispensation; above all, the exceeding goodness of giving us grounds for an assured persuasion that all is well with her; that she is gone to glory. When the hearse and our kind friends were gone, after a short time I came into my little room at the top of the stairs where I am now writing and engaged a while in prayer, blessing God for His astonishing goodness to me, and lamenting my extreme unworthiness.[5]

Emancipation

There was now only one cause he wanted to see begun in the House of Commons before he could retire in peace . . . the emancipation of all the slaves in the West Indies, and the remainder of the British Empire. Since abolition hadn't improved their conditions, he was now committed to campaigning for their full freedom. He announced as much to the Commons in 1822.

Beginning the Final Campaign

Not I only but all the chief advocates of the Aboli-tion declared from the first, that our object was by ameliorating regulations, and by stopping the influx of uninstructed savages, to advance slowly towards the period when these unhappy beings might exchange their degraded state of slavery for that of a free and industrious peasantry. To that most interesting object I still look forward, though perhaps of late we have all been chargeable with not paying due attention to the subject.[6]

He was confident of ultimate success, though he told to Macaulay, 'I own I am rather expecting that some convulsive and destructive spasms will accompany the violent death of this bloody monster.'[7] To ensure their success, he also that summer began a new regime of spiritual fitness.

Spiritual Plans

To-day I began the plan, to which by God's grace I mean to adhere, of having my evening private devotions before family prayers. For want of this they have too often been sadly hurried, and the reading of Scripture omitted. I have therefore resolved to allot an hour from half-past eight to half-past nine. It is a subtraction of the space to be allowed to business, but God seems to require it, and the grand, the only question is, what is God's will? The abridgement of my evening prayers has been a fault with me for years. May God help me to amend it, and give His blessing to a measure adopted with a view to please Him. Amen. Began to-day to keep a journal of time.[8]

That summer Lord Castlereagh committed suicide, and was replaced as Foreign Secretary by George Canning. It replaced an anti-abolition figure with an ally to the campaign. It also reinforced to Wilberforce the importance of his spiritual regime. He had now seen many in high office take their own lives due to the pressures they were under, and believed their workaholism had contributed to their deaths.

Benefits of a Sabbath

I must say that the occurrence of the same catastrophe, both to Whitbread, Romilly, and Londonderry [Castlereagh], has strongly enforced on my mind the unspeakable benefit of the institution of the Lord's day – for I don't like to call it the sabbath, as I do not quite consider it in the light in which it is viewed by many religious men. I am persuaded that to withdraw the mind one day in seven from its ordinary trains of thought and passion, and to occupy it in contemplating subjects of a higher order, which by their magnitude make worldly interests shrink into littleness, has the happiest effect on the intellectual and moral system. It gives us back on the Monday to the contemplation of our week-day business cooled and quieted, and it is to be hoped with resentments abated, and prejudices softened.[9]

Passing on the Leadership

He knew that he was now too old to take the lead role in what could be a long and difficult campaign. Happily, he had found a willing successor in Buxton, another independent, evangelical and passionate MP, and someone with youth on his side.

Buxton as Successor

Let me assure you . . . that I have often rejoiced of late years in thinking of my having you for an associate and successor, as indeed I told you. Now, my dear B., my remorse is sometimes very great, from my consciousness that we have not been duly active in endeavouring to put an end to that system of cruel bondage, which for two centuries has prevailed in our West Indian colonies; and my idea is, that a little before parliament meets, three or four of us should have a secret cabinet council, wherein we should deliberate and decide what cause to pursue. I can scarcely say what pain it would give me, were I to be unable before I go hence to declare my sentiments and feelings on this head.[10]

Preparing for Buxton and Macaulay, who came about four; I discussed with them on our plan . . . We must have a serious talk of the interior Cabinet, for the purpose of settling the measures to be recommended for preparing the slaves for the enjoyment of liberty. The Abolition of the driving system, with the introduction of religious instruction and marriage, and the facilitating manumissions [owners freeing slaves], must be, I cannot doubt, our grand measures.[11]

With Buxton the parliamentary leader, Macaulay repris-
ing his familiar role of faithful secretary sifting through
evidence, and incredibly the 62-year-old Thomas Clarkson once more mounting his horse to travel the country
and stir up anti-slavery societies, the campaign was born.
Wilberforce believed his best contribution could be a third
book, a criticism of slavery based on all the evidence he
had come across in thirty-six years' study of the subject.

A Third Book

I am now only beginning an undertaking which
ought by this time to have been finished . . . Really
when I consider the heathenish state in which those
poor creatures have been suffered to remain for two
hundred years, wearing out their strength in a far
more rigorous than Egyptian bondage to a Christian
nation; pity, anger, indignation, shame, create quite a
tumult in my breast, and I feel myself to be criminal for
having remained silent so long, and not having sooner
proclaimed the wrongs of the negro slaves, and the
injustice and oppression of our countrymen.[12]

He wrote it in three months, and it was published in
March 1823. One West Indian planter wrote to him, it 'has
so affected me, that should it cost me my whole property,
I surrender it willingly . . .'[13]

Wilberforce was again encouraged by the humanity of
the British people. 'It is wonderful how people accord with
us about the slaves; both government and West Indians.
May God bless our endeavours. The country takes up our
cause surprisingly. The petitions, considering the little
effort, very numerous.'[14]

On 15 May 1823 Buxton 'began his Slavery motion about half-past five. He moved a resolution declaring Slavery repugnant to Christianity and the constitution. Canning replied, and moved resolutions proclaiming reform of the system, and specifying driving, punishment of females, Sunday work, and market.'[15] It was a start. As ever, the campaign would work with those in power where it could, but came under increasing pressure to also call them to account when necessary.

Family Life

That summer he moved house again. '2nd [July 1823]. Took possession of our new house at Brompton Grove. May God bless our residence here.'[16] To Hannah More he explained, 'Marden Park was in one of the most beautiful countries eye ever beheld; but we were near three miles from church; we had no sheltered walk near the house, &c.'[17]

His family was also changing. All three youngest sons were now studying at Oxford, and applying themselves better than their elder brother had done. He regularly wrote with advice.

Fatherly Advice

Never omit any opportunity, my dear – , of getting acquainted with any good or useful man. More perhaps depends on the selection of acquaintance than on any other circumstance of life. Acquaintance are the raw material, from which are manufactured friends, husbands, wives. I wish it may please God that you may have some good ones to choose from on your first settling at Oxford.[18]

Final Parliament Activity

The situation was becoming more desperate in the West Indies. Many of the islands were experiencing insurrections as slaves demanded their freedom. Canning had tried to bring in gradual measures of improvement, but it had backfired, and he now blamed the campaigners. 'Mr Canning's private secretary stated that the insurrection in Demerara had been instigated by Wilberforce, Buxton, and Co.'[19] Wilberforce defended their campaign, and called again for full freedom of all slaves.

He also leant his weight to a final new cause, for an improvement in the treatment of animals. He became a founding Vice President of the Royal Society for the Prevention of Cruelty to Animals that was created in 1824.

Animal Rights Protector

March 1st [1824]. Went to the House for Martin's Bill on cruelty to animals. It is opposed on the ground of the rich having their own amusements, and that it would be hard to rob the poor of theirs – a most fallacious argument; and one which has its root in a contempt for the poor. I would zealously promote the real comfort of the poor.[20]

But his last Commons speeches were against slavery. In June 1824 he presented to parliament yet another petition on the subject. Ten days later he became seriously ill. His doctor and his family united in suggesting he retire from parliament, rather than put his recovery at risk. Like so many decisions before, he made a list to carefully weigh the pros and cons.

Reasons for Retiring from Parliament

- I have long meant to retire when this parliament should terminate; consequently, the only doubt is, whether to retire now, or at the end of the approaching session.

- The question then is, whether my qualified attendance during this session affords such a prospect of doing good as to warrant my continuance in parliament for its term?

- Dr Chambers does not deem it necessary to forbid my attendance altogether, but intimates fears that if an illness should occur, I might not have strength to stand it.

- Had I no other promising course of usefulness, it might or rather would be right to run the risk of a seizure, in my present line. But,

  1. I hope I may employ my pen to advantage if I retire into private life; and,

  2. My life is just now peculiarly valuable to my family – all at periods of life and in circumstances which render it extremely desirable, according to appearances, that I should be continued to them.

- I am not now much wanted in parliament; our cause has powerful advocates, who have now taken their stations.

- The example of a man's retiring when he feels his bodily and mental powers beginning to fail him, might probably be useful. The public have been so used to see persons turning a long-continued seat in parliament to account for obtaining rank, &c. that the contrary example the more needed, and it ought to be exhibited by one who professes to act on Christian principles.[21]

He chose to step down. Without any fanfare or ceremony, his political career had come to an end.

Retirement

In retirement he moved once more, to a property in Highwood Hill: 'We have bought a house about ten miles north of London. I shall be a little Zeminder there; 140 acres of land, cottages, of my own, &c.'[22] The land was used as a dairy farm. His son William, having tried and failed in a career as a lawyer, now decided to try his hand at farming. Wilberforce invested heavily to make the farm viable. He and Barbara lived there with William junior and family, plus the crowd of visitors and servants that accompanied Wilberforce wherever he went.

Account of Marianne Thornton

Things go on in the old way, the house thronged with servants who are all lame or impotent or blind, or kept from charity, an ex-secretary kept because he is grateful, and his wife because she nursed poor Barbara, and an old butler who they wish would not stay but then he is so attached, and his wife who was a cook but now she is so infirm. All this is rather as it should be, however, for one rather likes to see him so completely in character and would willingly despair of getting one's place changed at dinner and hear a chorus of

Bells all day which nobody answers for the sake of seeing Mr Wilberforce in his element.[23]

On 21 December 1825 he chaired the annual Anti-Slavery meeting in London, but decided he was too old to preside at such meetings. 'It seems like wishing to retain the reins, when I can no longer hold them.'[24] And when asked to continue lobbying the government through his private channels he confessed, 'I am a bee which has lost its sting.'[25] He stayed informed about the emancipation campaign, but came to disagree with some of the methods it was using – especially the concept of paying agents to work full time on the campaign, and the roles that women were taking on. He had been a great liberator for many, but in some respects he remained a traditionalist.

On Women as Campaigners

Macaulay giving me useful intelligence. We differing about Female Anti-Slavery Associations. Babington with me, grounding it on St Paul. I own I cannot relish the plan. All private exertions for such an object become their character, but for ladies to meet, to publish, to go from house to house stirring up petitions – these appear to me proceedings unsuited to the female character as delineated in Scripture.[26]

From April to October 1827 he made a trip to Yorkshire, in what he knew would be a final chance to see old friends. On his return he planned writing a new book on the Epistles of St Paul, or another chapter to his bestselling

Practical View of Real Christianity, but poor eyesight and failing health prevented either. His greatest pleasures were now found in the visits of friends and in walks through his garden. His early faith had partly come through seeing the majesty of the French and Swiss Alps, and now he again was moved to worship through even the smallest aspects of creation. 'Surely flowers are the smiles of His goodness.'[27]

He was treated as an elder statesman by those in the abolition movements, and by the various societies he had a hand in creating. He was always invited to their public meetings, but knew his days of making electrifying speeches were over.

Continued Activity

May 3rd [1828]. Freemason's Hall, Anti-Slavery meeting – Duke, Brougham, Denman, Mackintosh, &c. I could not get on comfortably or remember my topics.

6th. Church Missionary meeting, and the Report and motion falling in with my views, I pleased people. May it tend to augment the missionary spirit.

13th. Naval and Military Bible Society, where compelled to take the chair – delightful meeting.[28]

Such meetings were the exception rather than the rule. A more common day was, 'A solitary walk with the psalmist – evening quiet.'[29]

Losing His Fortune

Wilberforce had been comfortably rich throughout his life, and generous with the wealth God had given him. Now, at the end of his life, he lost his fortune.

William's farming career had not worked out. He took on debts which he hid from his father, and in 1830 he finally needed to be bailed out. Wilberforce had sold his old family home in Hull to pay the costs of setting up the farm. Now he needed to rescue his son from bankruptcy by selling the Highwood Hill home and farm. The man who had previously been rich enough to own several houses now owned none. He and Barbara spent the last years of his life living with their sons Robert and Samuel, both now ordained priests in the Anglican Church.

Letter to a Friend

The loss incurred has been so heavy as to compel me to descend from my present level, and greatly to diminish my establishment. But I am bound to recognize in this dispensation the gracious mitigation of the severity of the stroke. It was not suffered to take place till all my children were educated, and nearly all of them placed out in one way or another; and by the delay, Mrs Wilberforce and I are supplied with a delightful asylum under the roofs of two of our own children. And what better could we desire? A kind Providence has enabled me with truth to adopt the declaration of David, that goodness and mercy have followed me all my days. And now, when the cup presented to me has some bitter ingredients, yet surely no draught can be deemed distasteful which comes from such a hand,

and contains such grateful infusions as those of social intercourse and the sweet endearments of filial gratitude and affection. What I shall most miss will be my books and my garden . . .[30]

They travelled between the two sons, living alternately with one on the Isle of Wight, then with the other in Maidstone.

Cheerful in Adversity

We have now been here for about six weeks. How can I but rejoice rather than lament at a pecuniary loss, which has produced such a result as that of bringing us to dwell under the roofs of our dear children, and witness their enjoyment of a large share of domestic comforts, and their conscientious discharge of the duties of the most important of all professions.[31]

Soon after losing his home, his second daughter Elizabeth also died. Through the grief, he chose to find reasons to remain grateful.

The Death of Slavery

In April 1833 a Maidstone branch of the Anti-Slavery Society sent a petition to the House of Commons asking that slavery be outlawed. Wilberforce roused himself one last time to get to the public meeting and sign it. He spoke briefly about the evils of slavery and, as he did so, a shaft of sunlight came through the window of the room, as it had done back in 1792 when Pitt spoke against African slavery.

And as Pitt had done then, so now Wilberforce brought it into his speech: 'I trust that we now approach the very end of our career. The object is bright before us, the light of heaven beams on it, and is an earnest of success.'[32]

Rebellions in the West Indies made the government and the campaigners realize that emancipation was inevitable. Just weeks after the Maidstone meeting, parliament finally voted to abolish slavery throughout the British Empire. Macaulay wrote to Wilberforce with the news.

Letter from Macaulay

My dear Friend,
This day ten years ago the abolition of slavery was first made a question in Parliament. Last night its death-blow was struck. I send you a copy of the debate. Stanley's allusion to you was quite overpowering, and electrified the House. My dear friend, let me unite with you in thanks to God for this mercy.[33]

Wilberforce was now severely ill. Friends could see he was dying, and in July 1833 he travelled to London to see Dr Chambers, who had treated him during his 1824 illness. He was therefore in London as the third reading of the slavery debate took place. On 26 July the government agreed to full emancipation, and to giving out £20 million in total to compensate slave owners – 40 per cent of the annual government expenditure. Wilberforce rejoiced: 'Thank God, that I should have lived to witness a day in which England is willing to give twenty millions sterling for the Abolition of Slavery.'[34]

He died three days later, on 29 July 1833, with his wife and youngest son Henry with him.

Wilberforce's Final Words

Wilberforce: 'I am in a very distressed state.'
Henry: 'Yes, but you have your feet on the Rock.'
Wilberforce: 'I do not venture to speak so positively; but I hope I have.'[35]

He had planned to be buried in north London, alongside his sister Sarah, his daughter Barbara, and his great friend James Stephen. But on the day of his death, perhaps because his body was in London, and perhaps because of the legislation parliament had just passed, Lord Chancellor Henry Brougham came to Barbara Wilberforce with a request.

Honoured in Death

We, the undersigned, members of both Houses of Parliament, being anxious upon public grounds to show our respect for the memory of the late William Wilberforce, and being also satisfied that public honours can never be more fitly bestowed than upon such benefactors of mankind, earnestly request that he may be buried in Westminster Abbey; and that we, and others who may agree with us in these sentiments, may have permission to attend his funeral.[36]

He was buried one week later in Westminster Abbey, near the graves of Charles Fox and his great friend William Pitt.

James Stephen had died in October 1832, Hannah More died in September 1833, Zachary Macaulay died in 1838. The Clapham Sect passed away. Thomas Clarkson outlived them all. He died in 1846, and was the only one to see the full fruits of their campaigning, as on 1 August 1838, slavery died across the British Caribbean, and an estimated 800,000 people were given their freedom.

Free At Last

Key Learning Points

Spiritual Formation

Consider evening devotions. Most Christians have ordered devotions in the morning. Do you also need a regular time in the evening to connect with God?

Don't be a workaholic. Having a regular day off mitigates against this, and helps in adjusting to retirement.

Be open to friendships. Most of the good things in life come through relationships.

Don't discriminate. Wilberforce couldn't see the powerful roles that women could play in the campaign to end slavery. Don't use gender, age, ethnicity or anything else to blind yourself to what others can achieve.

Don't obsess over money. Use it to serve others, and then you won't miss it if it's ever taken away.

Discerning Vision

Think as well as pray when making decisions. Writing the pros and cons can help in discerning what to do.

Know when to retire. Don't continue on in leadership when others could do a better job than you.

Leadership Skills

Find a successor. But having found someone to take over your cause, continue to work with them. Do a proper handover to give them the best chance of success. Wilberforce shared with Buxton his connections, and the lessons learned from his previous campaigns.

Find other ways to contribute. Wilberforce couldn't lead a parliamentary campaign in the same way, but he could write a third book. Retirement from one role does not mean an end to all you can do.

INSTITUTE OF C
EMPLOYM

Please list all periods of employment,
employment should be explained.

Employer's name and address	D
	From

Endnotes

Works with multiple citations and their abbreviations:

Robert and Samuel Wilberforce, *Life of William Wilberforce in 5 Volumes* (London: John Murray, 1838) – abbr. to: *Life*

John S. Harford, *Recollections of William Wilberforce, Esq, MP for the County of York During Nearly Thirty Years* (London: Longmans, 1864) – abbr. to: Harford, *Recollections*

William Hague, *William Wilberforce* (London: HarperCollins, 2007) – abbr. to: Hague, *William Wilberforce*

Robert and Samuel Wilberforce, *The Correspondence of William Wilberforce in 2 Volumes* (Philadelphia: Perkins, 1841) – abbr. to: *Correspondence*

Chapter 1 – A Misspent Youth

[1] Robert and Samuel Wilberforce, *Life of William Wilberforce in 5 Volumes* (London: John Murray, 1838), Vol 1, p. 4

[2] John S. Harford, *Recollections of William Wilberforce, Esq, MP for the County of York During Nearly Thirty Years* (London: Longmans, 1864), p. 197–8

[3] *Life*, Vol 1, p. 7

[4] *Life*, Vol 1, p. 7

[5] *Life*, Vol 1, p. 7
[6] *Life*, Vol 1, p. 8
[7] *Life*, Vol 1, p. 6–7
[8] *Life*, Vol 1, p. 10
[9] *Life*, Vol 1, p. 10–11
[10] *Life*, Vol 1, p. 11
[11] *Life*, Vol 1, p. 12

Chapter 2 – A Man of Consequence

[1] Wilberforce Mss e.11 f.127, as cited in William Hague, *William Wilberforce* (London: HarperCollins, 2007), p. 24
[2] Wilberforce Mss c.43 f.5, as cited in Hague, *William Wilberforce*, p. 36
[3] *Life*, Vol 1, p. 16–17
[4] *Life*, Vol 1, p. 29
[5] *Life*, Vol 1, p. 30
[6] Letter to B.B. Thompson, 9 June 1781, from *Life*, Vol 1, p. 22
[7] *Life*, Vol 1, p. 18
[8] *Life*, Vol 1, p. 28
[9] *Life*, Vol 1, p. 29
[10] *Life*, Vol 1, p. 35
[11] *Life*, Vol 1, p. 36
[12] *Life*, Vol 1, p. 57
[13] *Life*, Vol 2, p. 133
[14] Letter from James Boswell to Henry Dundas, taken from *Life*, Vol 1, p. 54
[15] Taken from E. Metaxas, *Amazing Grace* (Oxford: Monarch Books, 2007), p. 39
[16] Rev. J. Pollock, *Wilberforce* (London: Constable & Co., 1977), as cited in Hague, *William Wilberforce*, p. 67
[17] Letter from William Pitt, 8 April 1784, from *Life*, Vol 1, p. 63

Chapter 3 – The Great Change

1. *Life*, Vol 1, p. 75
2. *Life*, Vol 1, p. 76
3. *Life*, Vol 1, p. 76
4. Harford, *Recollections*, p. 208
5. *Life*, Vol 1, p. 87
6. *Life*, Vol 1, p. 88–93
7. Harford, *Recollections*, p. 210
8. *Life*, Vol 1, p. 95
9. *Life*, Vol 1, p. 96
10. *Life*, Vol 1, p. 96–7
11. Harford, *Recollections*, p. 210
12. Letter from John Thornton, 24 December 1785, from *Life*, Vol 1, p. 104
13. *Life*, Vol 1, p. 104–5
14. *Life*, Vol 1, p. 119
15. Wilberforce Mss c.4 f.15–16, as cited in Hague, *William Wilberforce*, p. 101
16. Letter to Miss – , taken from Robert and Samuel Wilberforce, *The Correspondence of William Wilberforce in 2 Volumes* (Philadelphia: Perkins, 1841), Vol 1, p. 44
17. *Life*, Vol 1, p. 373
18. *Life*, Vol 1, p. 133–4
19. *Life*, Vol 1, p. 393
20. Letter from John Newton, 15 November 1786, from *Correspondence*, Vol 1, p. 14–15
21. *Life*, Vol 1, p. 149

Chapter 4 – The Trade in Flesh and Blood

1. *Life*, Vol 1, p. 148–9
2. A. Hochschild, *Bury The Chains* (London: Macmillan, 2005), p. 50

3   Hochschild, *Bury The Chains*, p. 81

4   Hochschild, *Bury The Chains*, p. 85

5   O. Equiano, *The Interesting Narrative* (London, 1789), p. 47

6   Equiano, *The Interesting Narrative*, p. 56–7

7   Equiano, *The Interesting Narrative*, p. 58

8   Equiano, *The Interesting Narrativ*, p. 104

9   Hochschild, *Bury The Chains*, p. 89

10 As cited in Hague, *William Wilberforce*, p. 136

11 As cited in Hague, *William Wilberforce*, p. 141

12 Harford, *Recollections*, p. 139

13 Letter from Granville Sharp, *Life*, Vol 1, p. 153

14 Hochschild, *Bury the Chains*, p. 110

15 Letter to Wyvill, from *Life*, Vol 1, p. 169–70

16 *Life*, Vol 1, p. 182

17 Letter from Newton, from *Correspondence*, Vol 1, p. 56, 58

18 *Life*, Vol 1, p. 198

19 *Life*, Vol 1, p. 206–8

20 *Life*, Vol 1, p. 213–4

Chapter 5 – The Early Debates

1   Illustration of Wedgwood medallion http://en.wikipedia. org/wiki/File:BLAKE10.JPG

2   http://www.geneseo.edu/~easton/engl313/CowperNC.html

3   'Stowage of the British Slave Ship *Brookes*' from: Regulated Slave Trade: From the Evidence of Robert Stokes, Esq., given before the Select Committee of the House of Lords, (London: J. Ridgway, 1851), http://rmc.library.cornell.edu/abolition-ism/origins/Slave_Ships.htm

4   *Life*, Vol 1, p. 218

5   As cited in Hague, *William Wilberforce*, p. 184

6   12 May 1789, *Parliamentary History of England, from the Earliest Period to the Year 1803* (London: Hansard, 1814), as cited in Hague, *William Wilberforce*, p. 179–83

7   *Life*, Vol 1, p. 235
8   William Loughton Smith, taken from Jay Winik, *The Great Upheaval* (London: Simon & Schuster, 2008), p. 167
9   *Life*, Vol 1, p. 229
10 *Life*, Vol 1, p. 240
11 Letter to Hannah More, from *Life*, Vol 1, p. 246–7
12 *Life*, Vol 1, p. 253–4
13 18 April 1791, Parliamentary History, as cited in Hague, *William Wilberforce*, p. 198
14 *Life*, Vol 1, p. 333–4
15 2 April 1792, Parliamentary History, as cited in Hague, *William Wilberforce*, p. 232
16 W.S. Hathaway, *The Speeches of the Right Honourable William Pitt in the House of Commons Vol 2* (London: Longman, 1806), as cited in William Hague, *William Pitt the Younger* (London: HarperCollins, 2004), p. 302–4
17 Letter to William Hey, 3 April 1792, from *Life*, Vol 1, p. 345–6
18 Letter to Gisborne, 10 April 1792, from *Life*, Vol 1, p. 348
19 Harford, *Recollections*, p. 141

Chapter 6 – Clapham Joy, Westminster Despair

1   Letter from Henry Thornton to Charles Grant, taken from Ernest M. Howse, *Saints in Politics* (London: George Allen & Unwin, 1973), p. 16.
2   John C. Colquhoun, William Wilberforce, His Friends and His Times, taken from Howse, *Saints in Politics*, p. 169–70
3   Letter to Gisborne, from *Life*, Vol 2, p. 27
4   *Life*, Vol 1, p. 357
5   *Life*, Vol 1, p. 359
6   Letter from Mr Clarke, from *Life*, Vol 2, p. 18
7   *Life*, Vol 2, p. 114
8   *Life*, Vol 2, p. 139–140
9   *Life*, Vol 2, p. 141

10 *Life*, Vol 2, p. 141–2
11 *Life*, Vol 2, p. 142
12 *Life*, Vol 2, p. 199
13 William Wilberforce, *A Practical View of Christianity* (Massachusetts: Hendrickson Publishers, 1996) p. 181–2, 184–5, 187
14 Wilberforce, *A Practical View of Christianity*, p. 176
15 Letter from Muncaster, from *Life*, Vol 2, p. 199–200
16 Letter from Newton, 21 April 1797 from *Correspondence*, Vol 1, p. 156
17 *Life*, Vol 2, p. 201
18 *Life*, Vol 2, p. 202–3
19 *Life*, Vol 2, p. 208
20 *Life*, Vol 2, p. 210
21 *Life*, Vol 2, p. 214
22 *Life*, Vol 2, p. 220–1

Chapter 7 – Outside Interests

1 *Life*, Vol 2, p. 251
2 *Life*, Vol 2, p. 260
3 *Life*, Vol 2, p. 265
4 *Life*, Vol 2, p. 265–6
5 W.S. Hathaway, *The Speeches of the Right Honourable William Pitt in the House of Commons*, Vol 3, as cited in William Hague, *William Pitt the Younger* (London: HarperCollins, 2004), p. 425
6 Letter from Pitt, from *Life*, Vol 2, p. 281
7 *Life*, Vol 2, p. 254
8 *Life*, Vol 2, p. 275–6
9 Letter from Henry Thornton to Hannah More, 30 October 1799, from *Life*, Vol 2, p. 350
10 *Life*, Vol 2, p. 277
11 *Life*, Vol 3, p. 3
12 Letter to William Hey, 25 February 1801, from *Life*, Vol 3, p. 5
13 Letter to Hannah More, 7 September 1802, from *Life*, Vol 3, p.

67–8
14 *Life*, Vol 3, p. 48–9
15 *Life*, Vol 3, p. 88
16 R. Steer, *Good News for the World: The Story of the Bible Society* (Oxford: Monarch, 2004), p. 54
17 *Life*, Vol 3, p. 91
18 *Life*, Vol 3, p. 91
19 Steer, *Good News for the World*, p. 56

Chapter 8 – West Indian Abolition

1 *Life*, Vol 3, p. 168
2 *Life*, Vol 3, p. 176
3 *Life*, Vol 3, p. 177
4 Letter to John Newton , from *Life*, Vol 3, p. 170
5 Letter to Lord Grenville, 27 June 1804, from *Life*, Vol 3, p. 179
6 *Life*, Vol 3, p. 180–1
7 Letter to Gisborne, 28 June 1804, from *Life*, Vol 3, p. 181
8 Letter to Muncaster, 6 July 1804, from *Life*, Vol 3, p. 182
9 *Life*, Vol 3, p. 184
10 Letter to Pitt, 14 September 1804, from *Correspondence*, Vol 1, p. 311–12
11 *Life*, Vol 3, p. 212
12 *Life*, Vol 3, p. 213
13 *Life*, Vol 3, p. 213
14 R. Furneaux, *William Wilberforce* (London: Hamish Hamilton, 1974), as cited in Hague, *William Wilberforce*, p. 323
15 *Life*, Vol 3, p. 229–30
16 Letter to Muncaster, 25 January 1806, from *Life*, Vol 3, p. 245
17 *Life*, Vol 3, p. 261
18 *Life*, Vol 3, p. 262–3
19 10 June 1806, *Parliamentary Debates from the Year 1803 to the Present Time* (London: Hansard, 1812), as cited in Hague, *William Wilberforce*, p. 340

[20] *Life*, Vol 3, p. 263

[21] *Life*, Vol 3, p. 273

[22] *Life*, Vol 3, p. 295

[23] As cited in Metaxas, *Amazing Grace*, p. 209–10

[24] *Life*, Vol 3, p. 298

[25] Letter to Stephen, 24 February 1807, from *Life*, Vol 3, p. 298–9

[26] *Life*, Vol 3, p. 305

[27] *Life*, Vol 3, p. 303

[28] *Life*, Vol 3, p. 338–9

[29] *Life*, Vol 3, p. 341–2

Chapter 9 – East Indian Victory

[1] *Life*, Vol 3, p. 351–2

[2] *Life*, Vol 3, p. 235

[3] *Life*, Vol 3, p. 387

[4] *Life*, Vol 3, p. 470

[5] *Life*, Vol 3, p. 393

[6] *Life*, Vol 3, p. 446

[7] Harford, *Recollections*, p. 109

[8] *Life*, Vol 3, p. 397

[9] *Life*, Vol 3, p. 374

[10] *Life*, Vol 3, p. 486–7

[11] *Life*, Vol 3, p. 535

[12] *Life*, Vol 3, p. 537

[13] *Life*, Vol 4, p. 5

[14] *Life*, Vol 4, p. 13

[15] *Life*, Vol 4, p. 26

[16] *Life*, Vol 4, p. 95

[17] *Life*, Vol 4, p. 112

[18] Letter to Hannah More, March 1813, from *Life*, Vol 4, p. 103

[19] *Life*, Vol 4, p. 112

[20] *Life*, Vol 4, p. 116–7

[21] *Life*, Vol 4, p. 118

22 *Life*, Vol 4, p. 120
23 Ernest M. Howse, *Saints in Politics* (London: George Allen & Unwin, 1973), p. 88–91
24 1 July 1813, *Parliamentary Debates*, as cited in Hague, *William Wilberforce*, p. 411
25 *Life*, Vol 4, p. 124–5
26 Letter to Muncaster, 2 September 1813, from *Correspondence*, Vol 2, p. 271

Chapter 10 – An International Campaigner

1 *Life*, Vol 4, p. 161–2
2 *Life*, Vol 4, p. 187
3 *Life*, Vol 4, p. 190–1
4 Letter to Macaulay, 3 August 1814, from *Life*, Vol 4, p. 209–10
5 Letter from Henry Thornton to Hannah More, 2 December 1814, from *Life*, Vol 4, p. 221–2
6 Letter from Lord Castlereagh, 31 July 1815, from *Life*, Vol 4, p. 224
7 *Life*, Vol 4, p. 231
8 *Life*, Vol 4, p. 365–6
9 *Life*, Vol 4, p. 249
10 S. Tomkins, *The Clapham Sect* (Oxford: Lion Hudson, 2010), p. 209
11 Letter to Lord Liverpool, 17 March 1815, from *Life*, Vol 4, p. 252
12 Letter to Macaulay, 27 January 1817, from *Life*, Vol 4, p. 307
13 *Life*, Vol 4, p. 310
14 *Life*, Vol 4, p. 345–7
15 Letter to Zachary Macaulay, 9 October 1817 from *Life*, Vol 4, p. 330
16 *Life*, Vol 4, p. 354
17 *Life*, Vol 4, p. 368
18 *Life*, Vol 4, p. 376

[19] *Life*, Vol 4, p. 277
[20] *Life*, Vol 4, p. 277
[21] *Life*, Vol 5, p. 57
[22] *Life*, Vol 5, p. 58
[23] *Life*, Vol 5, p. 66
[24] *Life*, Vol 5, p. 68
[25] Letter to James Stephen, 29 October 1820, from *Life*, Vol 5, p. 79–80

Chapter 11 – Free At Last

[1] *Life*, Vol 5, p. 95
[2] *Life*, Vol 5, p. 100
[3] *Life*, Vol 5, p. 101
[4] *Life*, Vol 5, p. 107
[5] *Life*, Vol 5, p. 111–2
[6] *Life*, Vol 5, p. 131
[7] *Life*, Vol 5, p. 125
[8] *Life*, Vol 5, p. 131–2
[9] *Life*, Vol 5, p. 143
[10] Letter to Thomas Buxton, 6 December 1822, from *Life*, Vol 5, p. 157
[11] *Life*, Vol 5, p. 162–3
[12] Letter to Lady Olivia Sparrow, 22 January 1823, from *Life*, Vol 5, p. 164–5
[13] *Life*, Vol 5, p. 168
[14] *Life*, Vol 5, p. 176–7
[15] *Life*, Vol 5, p. 177
[16] *Life*, Vol 5, p. 187
[17] Letter to Hannah More, July 1823, from *Life*, Vol 5, p. 188
[18] Letter to his son, 14 June 1823, from *Life*, Vol 5, p. 184
[19] *Life*, Vol 5, p. 201
[20] *Life*, Vol 5, p. 213–4
[21] *Life*, Vol 5, p. 233–4

22 Letter to Gisborne, 6 April 1825, from *Life*, Vol 5, p. 248
23 E.M. Forster, *Marianne Thornton* (London: Edward Arnold, 1956), as cited in Hague, *William Wilberforce*, p. 491–2
24 Letter to Babington, 1 December 1826, from *Life*, Vol 5, p. 263
25 *Life*, Vol 5, p. 263
26 *Life*, Vol 5, p. 264
27 *Life*, Vol 5, p. 287
28 *Life*, Vol 5, p. 300
29 *Life*, Vol 5, p. 311
30 Letter to a friend, 16 March 1831, from *Life*, Vol 5, p. 325–6
31 Letter to James Stephen, from *Life*, Vol 5, p. 331
32 Life, Vol 5, p. 354
33 Letter from Zachary Macaulay, from *Correspondence*, Vol 2, p. 331
34 Letter to Zachary Macaulay, from *Life*, Vol 5, p. 370
35 *Life*, Vol 5, p. 373
36 Harford, *Recollections*, p. 249–50

Bibliography

Edwards, Brian H., *Through Many Dangers: The Story of John Newton* (London: Evangelical Press, 1975)

Equiano, Olaudah, *An Interesting Narrative and Other Writings* (London, Penguin Classics, 2003)

Fendall, Lon, *William Wilberforce: Abolitionist, Politician, Writer* (Ohio: Barbour Books, 2002)

Hague, William, *William Pitt the Younger* (London: Harper Perennial, 2005)

Hague, William, *William Wilberforce* (London: Harper Perennial, 2008)

Harford, John S., *Recollections of William Wilberforce Esq, MP for the County of York During Nearly Thirty Years* (London: Forgotten Books, 2012)

Hill, Clifford, *The Wilberforce Connection* (Oxford: Monarch Books, 2004)

Hochschild, Adam, *Bury The Chains* (London: Pan MacMillan, 2006)

Howse, Ernest Marshall, *Saints in Politics* (London: George Allen & Unwin, 1971)

Metaxas, Eric, *Amazing Grace* (Oxford: Monarch Books, 2007)

Piper, John, *Amazing Grace in the Life of William Wilberforce* (Nottingham: IVP, 2007)

Steer, Roger, *Good News for the World: The Story of the Bible Society* (Oxford: Monarch Books, 2004)

Tomkins, Stephen, *The Clapham Sect* (Oxford: Lion Hudson, 2010)

Wilberforce, Robert Isaac and Samuel Wilberforce, eds., *The Life of William Wilberforce,* 5 volumes (London: John Murray, 1838)

Wilberforce, Robert Isaac and Samuel Wilberforce, eds., *The Correspondence of William Wilberforce,* 2 volumes (Cambridge: Cambridge University Press, 2010)

Wilberforce, William, *A Practical View of Christianity* (Massachusetts: Hendrickson Publishers, 1996)

Winik, Jay, *The Great Upheaval* (London: Simon & Schuster, 2008)

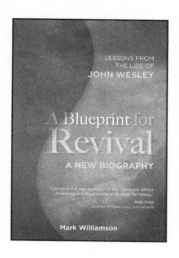

A Blueprint for Revival

Lessons from the Life of John Wesley

Mark Williamson

For centuries God has used committed men and women to share his love, lead his people and shape his Church. Whether they feature in the Bible or have been serving God in more recent times we can learn so much from the many leaders and servants who have gone before.

John Wesley was one of the UK's great leaders, whose passion for God led him to do amazing things. *A Blueprint for Revival* clearly lays out the key moments of Wesley's story, using journal extracts, letters and writings to give insight into both the personal and professional aspects of his life. From the influence of his parents to his time at Oxford, from his founding of Methodism to his handling of relationships, this book shows us a man who was dedicated, disciplined and devout.

978-1-85078-962-8

Going Forward on Your Knees

Lessons from the Life of Hudson Taylor

Joanna E. Williamson

For centuries God has used committed men and women to share his love, lead his people and shape his Church. Whether they feature in the Bible or have been serving God in more recent times we can learn so much from the many leaders and servants who have gone before.

Going Forward on Your Knees tells the story of Hudson Taylor's life using many of his own words, drawing us right into his world. He is one of the most inspirational Christians of all time. An early missionary to China, he overcame significant obstacles – poor health, shortage of money and language issues. He went on to found his own mission organization, the China Inland Mission (now OMF International).

978-1-85078-961-1

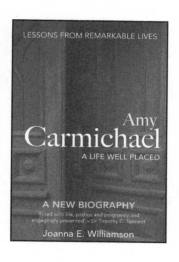

Amy Carmichael

A Life Well Placed

Joanna E. Williamson

Amy Carmichael was a remarkable leader. She lived her life out of a strong belief in a God who is real, all powerful and who provides for all our needs. She had a deep love for people and a determination to help them. She provided a home, an education and health care for hundreds of girls and boys whom she rescued from moral and physical danger. The Dohnavur Fellowship she established survived two world wars, outbreaks of disease and persistent spiritual attack. She authored nearly 40 books that continue to inspire and nourish the souls of many.

This book is part of the Remarkable Lives series of biographies from One Rock, each designed to do three things: tell the life story of a remarkable Christian missionary, act as a reference work featuring that person's most important quotes and anecdotes, and serve as a training tool through the key learning points at the end of each chapter.

978-1-78078-062-7

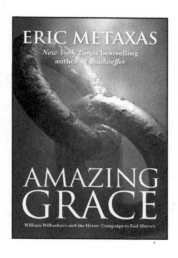

Amazing Grace

William Wilberforce and the Heroic Campaign to End Slavery

Eric Metaxas

In *Amazing Grace*, Eric Metaxas's gripping narrative paints a detailed portrait, not just of William Wilberforce himself and the Abolitionist Movement but also other contemporary concerns of the social reformers. Together with entries from Wilberforce's own diaries documenting his travels and the people he meets – from the paupers of Cheddar to Marie Antoinette – this age is brought vividly to life.

978-1-78078-304-8